BrightRED Study Guide

Curriculum for Excellence

N5

DRAMA

Samantha MacDonald

BrightRED
PUBLISHING

First published in 2014 by:
Bright Red Publishing Ltd
1 Torphichen Street
Edinburgh
EH3 8HX

Reprinted with corrections in 2017

A CIP record for this book is available from the British Library

ISBN 978-1-906736-53-8

With thanks to:
PDQ Digital Media Solutions Ltd (layout), Sue Moody, Bright Writing (edit)

Cover design and series book design by Caleb Rutherford – e i d e t i c

Acknowledgements
Every effort has been made to seek all copyright holders. If any have been overlooked, then Bright Red Publishing will be delighted to make the necessary arrangements.

Permission has been sought from all relevant copyright holders and Bright Red Publishing are grateful for the use of the following:
shvili/iStock.com (p 6); 123foto/iStock.com (p 9); C. Thomas Anderson (CC BY-SA 2.0)[1] (p 11); Mardi Gras (CC BY 2.0)[2] (p 11); Chris Brown (CC BY-SA 2.0)[1] (p 11); Keoni Cabral (CC BY 2.0)[2] (p 11); Artist2000 (CC BY-SA 3.0)[3] (p 11); Camille Pissarro, Le Jardin de Mirbeau aux Damps (public domain) (p 11); Cassatt Mary 'Girl Arranging Her Hair' 1886 (public domain) (p 11); Gavin Schaefer (CC BY 2.0)[2] (p 13); Angela Thomas (CC BY 2.0)[2] (p 14); Jenna Carver (CC BY 2.0)[2] (p 17); Laura Kishimoto (p 18); Image from 'A Taste of Honey' by Shelagh Delaney, featuring Traci Asaurus and Maynard Okereke, at Eclectic Theater © Scott Maddock (p 18); Image from 'The Importance of Being Ernest' by Oscar Wilde © Department of Theatre, Harding University, Searcy, AR, USA (p 18); Vancouver Film School (CC BY 2.0)[2] (pp 20 & 21); Caleb Rutherford/e i d e t i c (p 22); Eva Rinaldi (CC BY-SA 2.0)[1] (p 23); Anthony Topper (CC BY 2.0)[2] (p 24); Image from 'Black Watch' 2012 © Manuel Harlan/National Theatre of Scotland (p 25); Wen-Cheng Liu (CC BY-SA 2.0)[1] (p 27); Phil Kahlina (CC BY 2.0)[2] (p 28); Barry Solow (CC BY-SA 2.0)[1] (p 29); Sintez/iStock.com (p 31); Dslaven/Dreamstime.com (p 32); liseykina/iStock.com (p 34); Tomwang112/iStock.com (p 35); Image from 'Romeo and Juliet' at Hart House Theatre © Daniel DiMarco (p 36); Julie Lush (p 37); Petr Mika (CC BY 2.0)[2] (p 38); Tambako The Jaguar (CC BY-ND 2.0)[3] (p 40); Vanmapse/Dreamstime.com (p 41); yaruta/iStock.com (p 42); Luso/iStock.com (p 42); Erin Kohlenberg (CC BY 2.0)[2] (p 43); baona/iStock.com (p 44); Insomnia Cured Here (CCBY-SA 2.0)[1] (p 45); Sheena876 (CC BY-SA 2.0)[1] (p 46); Ryan Hyde (CC BY-SA 2.0)[1] (p 47); Ansel Edwards (CC BY 2.0)[2] (p 47); Sukanto Debnath (CC BY 2.0)[2] (p 47); Abhishek Kumar (CC BY 2.0)[2] (p 49); Vancouver Film School (CC BY 2.0)[2] (p 51); Alexandre Delbos (CC BY 2.0)[2] (p 52); IPGGutenbergUKLtd/iStock.com (p 56); Nic McPhee (CC BY 2.0)[2] (p 58); Sarah Sierszyn (CC BY 2.0)[2] (p 58); Denise Curran (CC BY 2.0)[2] (p 59); Alfredo Cofré (CC BY-SA 2.0)[1] (p 59); David R. Tribble (CC BY-SA 3.0)[3] (p 60); Mark Ordonez (CC BY-SA 2.0)[1] (p 60); foam (CC BY-SA 2.0)[1] (p 61); Jef Kratochvil (CC BY-SA 3.0 CZ)[5] (p 63); VvoeVale/iStock.com (p 64); rilueda/iStock.com (p 64); Mickey Thurman (CC BY 2.0)[2] (p 66); joshdbrown (CC BY 2.0)[2] (p 66); leszekglasner/iStock.com (p 66); Marcus Meissner (CC BY 2.0)[2] (p 66); Image from 'Black Watch' 2012 © Manuel Harlan/National Theatre of Scotland (p 68); jackfoto/iStock.com (p 70); Vancouver Film School (CC BY 2.0)[2] (pp 72 & 73); Amanda Bowman (CC BY-ND 2.0)[3] (p 75); Two images by MCAD Library (CC BY 2.0)[2] (p 76); Kristen Taylor (CC BY-SA 2.0)[1] (p 77); Steven Depolo (CC BY 2.0)[2] (p 78); Jonathan Kos-Read (CC BY-ND 2.0)[3] (p 79); DonNichols/iStock.com (p 81); Morgan (CC BY 2.0)[2] (p 82); Thomas Kohler (CC BY-SA 2.0)[1] (p 83); Pedro Cambra (CC BY 2.0)[2] (p 84); Jason W (CC BY 2.0)[2] (p 84); koya79/iStock.com (p 86); aerogondo/iStock.com (p 87); Michael Pollak (CC BY 2.0)[2] (p 88); © typofi/freeimages.com (p 90); BlueJames/iStock.com (p 91).

(CC BY-SA 2.0)[1] http://creativecommons.org/licenses/by-sa/2.0/
(CC BY 2.0)[2] http://creativecommons.org/licenses/by/2.0/
(CC BY-ND 2.0)[3] http://creativecommons.org/licenses/by-nd/2.0/
(CC BY-SA 3.0)[4] http://creativecommons.org/licenses/by-sa/3.0/
(CC BY-SA 3.0 CZ)[5] http://creativecommons.org/licenses/by-sa/3.0/cz/

Printed and bound in the UK.

CONTENTS LIST

INTRODUCING NATIONAL 5 DRAMA

STUDYING DRAMA

Drama is a creative subject and great fun to study. Throughout this course you will have opportunities to develop skills in creating and presenting drama to an audience. It is not just the final production that matters however, but also the entire process of developing a production.

You will learn many new skills and refine some you already have, but the most important skill in studying drama by far is working with others. Almost everything you do in this course will involve working collaboratively in some way, and your level of success will largely depend on your ability to communicate and negotiate in a group situation. Try to bear this in mind throughout the process and above all be flexible and creative in how you approach working in a team.

The course aims are to enable learners to:

- generate and communicate thoughts and ideas when creating drama
- develop a knowledge and understanding of a range of social and cultural influences on drama
- develop a range of skills in presenting drama
- develop knowledge, understanding and the use of a range of production skills when presenting drama
- explore form, structure, genre and style.

The purpose of the National 5 Drama course is to enable you to develop and use a range of drama and production skills.

DRAMA SKILLS

Throughout the course you will have opportunities to develop your drama skills through contributing to the drama process. You will work with others to respond to **stimuli** – including **text** – to generate ideas for drama and devise performances. You will experiment with drama skills to:

- communicate ideas to an audience
- use a range of acting skills and **characterisation** techniques
- explore **form**, **genre**, **structure** and **style**
- gain experience of evaluating your own work and that of others.

DRAMA: PRODUCTION SKILLS

During your course you will also have an opportunity to focus on the skills required to contribute to a production. You will have the opportunity to learn about a variety of production roles and how they contribute to a performance. You will be required to work with others to generate ideas for a **production concept** and to analyse and apply a range of production skills. These could include lighting, **costume**, sound, **props**, set design and make-up.

The National 5 Drama course is externally assessed through a question paper and a performance.

QUESTION PAPER

The question paper is carried out under exam conditions. It lasts 1 hour and 30 minutes and is worth 60 marks which make up 40% of the overall course award. There are two sections: an evaluation worth 20 marks and a response to a stimulus for 40 marks.

EVALUATION

The evaluation will involve you answering questions to evaluate your contribution to a production. You can choose any production you have been part of during your course in either an acting or a production role.

Be prepared to answer questions about your intended audience for the production and your thinking behind the aims of the production. Think about how you wanted the audience to feel or react and the mood and atmosphere you aimed to create. You will also be asked to evaluate how successfully this was achieved. Remember to justify everything you say with evidence or examples and don't be afraid to highlight areas for improvement. As long as you can explain why something was not quite as successful as you would have liked and how you would develop this in future it is useful evaluation and will be awarded marks.

To prepare for this, it is useful to practise evaluating your own and others' work throughout your course in a logbook or blog. See the sections on recording evidence for more on this (pp 64–5 and 90–91).

RESPONSE TO A STIMULUS

The response to a stimulus section will involve you creating ideas for a dramatic performance inspired by one of the given **stimuli**. There will be a choice of stimuli which could include a photograph, a phrase, a newspaper headline, an extract from a script or an object. You will be asked to choose one of the stimuli and to generate ideas for a performance.

This section will include questions about process, performance and production elements. You will need to be able to describe and justify your intentions behind the production, such as the main theme or message. You might be asked about the **rehearsal techniques** you would use, the structure of the narrative, design elements such as lighting or costume, **theatre conventions** you would include and so on.

Again, you must justify every choice you make. For example, it is not enough to simply describe what you would like your set to look like. You must explain why you have made this choice in terms of how it adds to the production. Does it add to the overall mood or feel of the piece? Does it allow for the right kind of movement around the performance space?

ONLINE

You can see an example question paper at www. brightredbooks.net/N5Drama

PERFORMANCE

The performance is worth 60 marks (and 60% of the overall course award): 50 marks for the performance itself and 10 marks for the preparation of the performance. You will be assessed on the preparation and performance of an extract of text for an audience. The performance should last between 10 and 50 minutes depending on the number of people performing. There should be a minimum of two performers and a maximum of ten. Not all performers need to be assessed. You can choose an acting or a production role for the performance.

If you choose a production role for the performance, you will need to demonstrate your design or concept for the production through drawings, designs and/or mood boards. You will also need to demonstrate the practical realisation of your design or concept in the performance.

PREPARATION OF PERFORMANCE

This will provide evidence of your research and thinking behind the performance. It should demonstrate the reasons for the choice of text to perform, your research into the text, your interpretation of the text, your role and the process you went through to design your concept. For more on this, read the Assessment chapter on pages 84–95.

THINGS TO DO AND THINK ABOUT

There is a great deal of freedom in this largely practical course to make your own choices and decisions about what direction to take the drama and how to progress through the course. Reflect often on your learning and challenge yourself to develop new skills.

The 'Things to Do and Think About' section in every chapter contains useful suggestions for you to try throughout your course. The activities will help you to develop and practise your drama and production skills as you progress through the course. They can be used as introductory or warm-up activities or help with rehearsals and performances.

WORKING WITH OTHERS – SHARING IDEAS AND PLANNING

Collaborative working is an essential element of National 5 Drama. You will be working with others most of the time during the course so it is vital to develop good collaboration skills. The better your group-work skills, the better you will do in your course, as planning your production will involve a great deal of group discussion. You shouldn't try to take over or take a back seat, but aim to strike a balance between the two. Offer your own ideas and support others to offer theirs also.

TOP TIPS FOR WORKING WITH OTHERS

LET GO OF YOUR EGO

Don't take things personally. Even if your idea is rejected by the group, try to think about what is best for the drama. If you continue coming up with ideas, the chances are that some of them will make it into the performance. Take criticism graciously and see it as helping you to improve.

BE PATIENT

Remember that everyone thinks and learns in different ways. Even if something appears clear to you, it might be more difficult for someone else. Try to be supportive of your team.

BE CALM

Control your emotions in discussions. Drama can be an emotional experience, but keep it in perspective. Try to argue your case logically and reasonably and then move on.

LISTEN

Remember that everyone wants to be listened to. Give others the consideration you would like them to give you. If you listen to others, they will be more inclined to listen to you.

BE KIND

Some are more confident than others in contributing their ideas. Think about having all members of the group write down their ideas anonymously and put them into a hat. Take turns to read out the ideas until all have been read. This means those who are less confident will get to contribute their ideas in a safe way.

contd

NEGOTIATE

Practise negotiation skills by role-playing difficult situations with infuriating characters. Everyone experiences times when they have to work with people they find difficult. Being able to negotiate effectively with people is a great skill that is worth developing. Try role-playing situations where you have to deal with a difficult customer or someone who constantly puts you down. You have to be assertive but not aggressive and send them away happy.

BE AWARE

Try to be aware of the reasons why people might be difficult or upset. Often people struggle when they are out of their comfort zone. Can you offer some kind of support to make it less scary for them? If people feel overlooked or think they have been given the worst role, they can react negatively.

AGREE

Decide at the beginning of the process on some rules or guidelines for the group. For example, you might agree beforehand that decisions will be made by vote and the majority rules. Or that one person (perhaps the teacher or another person taking the role of director) has the final say. All members of the group have to honour this decision, with no hard feelings – even if their idea is not chosen.

DEALING WITH DISAGREEMENTS

- If a discussion is not working and you find yourselves going round and round in circles getting frustrated, try a different approach. Stop discussing and get up and try things out.

- If you cannot agree on an idea or an approach, try both and see which works best. Try to keep an open mind and embrace the ideas of others.

- If a consensus cannot be reached, the only option might be to combine two ideas. This can sometimes lead to very creative solutions that would not otherwise have been considered.

- Above all, communicate – and communicate often. Don't expect your group to know what you are thinking if you haven't communicated it. Update each other on progress in research or in generating ideas regularly.

THINGS TO DO AND THINK ABOUT

1. Write a list of guidelines for good group working. Think about your ideal working situation and try to describe it. This will help when you start to negotiate ground rules. If everyone in the group does this, the chances are you will find that you agree on many points.

2. Try out some bonding activities with your group before you begin working together. These are a good way to establish good relationships and discover each other's talents. Games where the whole group has to work together to achieve an aim, or games where everyone looks a bit silly and falls about laughing are good ones to go for.

3. The counting game is a simple way to start. Everyone in the group closes their eyes or stands in a circle with their backs to the centre. You must then count to 20 as a group, with one person saying each number. If two or more people say the same number, you have to start all over again. Don't give up – it is possible and it takes practice!

DON'T FORGET

You are working as a team. The better your teamwork, the better your performance will be.

DON'T FORGET

Criticism is an opportunity to improve. Remember that this is a learning process and you can challenge yourself to be the best you can be.

ONLINE

For more tips about group working, head to www.brightredbooks.net/N5Drama

ONLINE TEST

How well have you learned about working with others? Test yourself online at www.brightredbooks.net/N5Drama

AUDIENCE

There is no show without an audience, so they are an extremely important consideration in your work. Developing a drama or theatre production is like writing, in that you need (if possible) to know your audience before you start so that the material, styles and language you choose for your piece are appropriate and relevant for that specific group. It is possible that some groups will identify with certain themes while others will not. Some might be offended by certain language while others will not, and certain stories might be more appropriate for some age groups and not others. Understanding your audience goes a long way to making a successful production.

ONLINE

Have a look at the upcoming shows from different theatres – there are links to some at www. brightredbooks.net/N5Drama – and see if you can easily spot the differences in plays aimed at each of these different groups.

WHAT IS YOUR AIM?

Above all, think about your aim for the audience experience. What do you want them to think/feel? Do you want to leave them wondering about something, or to be uplifted by a happy ending? Do you want them to start believing one thing and then change their minds? Do you want to surprise or shock them?

WHO ARE THEY AND WHAT DOES THAT MEAN?

For each group, you must think about their expectations. What will their experience of theatre be and what will you need to explain?

VERY YOUNG CHILDREN

Small children can have short attention spans, so think about the length of your production. They will have very limited experience of being an audience, so they will have no expectations and will probably get involved if you invite them to. Think about how you will manage that, as they might not behave as you expect.

Keep your story simple or familiar and bear in mind that children respond to bright colours, song and dance and funny characters. They might cry or interrupt, so think about disruptive behaviour and how you would cope with that. Think, too, about any parents present. If their children enjoy the performance, most adults will be happy, but you could throw in some jokes or **asides** for the adults to keep them entertained.

PRIMARY-AGE CHILDREN

Primary-age children will have higher expectations because they will already have seen some productions and they will know how to be an audience. They might be quite shy and need encouragement to get involved individually, but they will enjoy joining in as a group with things like pantomime-style responses and song actions.

Older primary students will enjoy more complex stories with challenging themes.

YOUNG TEENAGERS/TWEENS

Be careful not to patronise young teenagers because they can consider themselves quite sophisticated, but be careful, too, about including adult themes. This age group will be familiar with a variety of **theatre forms** and will have certain expectations of the form you choose. They are often quite self-conscious about participating individually, but will probably respond as a group. They will enjoy references to popular culture in your story.

YOUNG ADULTS/TEENAGERS

This age group can understand very sophisticated stories and will probably have some background knowledge of literature and politics. They will have a fair amount of experience and certain expectations of theatre forms. Teenagers often enjoy challenging social themes and references to subculture. Generally, this age group is quite reluctant to get involved with **audience participation**.

ADULTS

Adults will have a varied experience of theatre forms and will come to the performance with expectations, but might enjoy having those expectations challenged. Adults can usually be persuaded to get involved in audience participation if you pitch it right.

COMMUNICATING WITH THE AUDIENCE

WHERE ARE THEY?

In rehearsals, always think about where the audience is. This will partially depend upon the **staging** you are using, but it's important to know this at the beginning of the rehearsal process because, for example, your approach to **proscenium arch** staging will be different to **in the round** staging. Have a look at the section on staging (pp 66–67) for more information about this.

CONNECT

Even if you are not directly addressing the audience in your performance, everything you do is about communicating with them. They have to be able to see, hear and understand what is going on. You are responsible for making sure they can, so it is very important to think about how you are communicating with them. Use your voice and **body language** to connect with the audience. Don't give them your back or speak to the floor.

NARRATING

Narrating is a skill that is used to develop a relationship with the audience. Think about your voice and body language and how you use it to get and keep their attention. Are you a friendly narrator? Are you sharing jokes with them? Maybe your job is to get them excited or heighten the tension? Make sure you bring everybody in when narrating and don't address only one section of the audience. Vary your eyeline so everyone feels as if you are speaking to them.

BREACHING THE FOURTH WALL

If you want an element of audience participation in your production, think carefully about how you manage this. It can be a tricky thing to do as you are introducing an element of uncertainty into your show. Will the audience react as you expect them to? You need to be able to maintain an element of control.

There are various levels of audience participation. Think about what would work best for your purposes:
- They stay in their seats and you encourage them to respond as a group.
- They stay in their seats and you choose individuals to respond.
- You invite individuals into the performance.
- The audience members are free to get involved whenever they choose.
- The audience members are integral to the performance and have a large degree of influence over what happens.

It is a skill to get people involved, and you need to be sensitive to the audience's expectations and their willingness to join in. If they are uncertain, you need to be supportive and encouraging. Most people will feel okay about responding as a group if it is very clear what is expected of them. If you are looking for an individual, look for someone who makes eye contact and is smiling. Those who don't want to get involved will look away.

THINGS TO DO AND THINK ABOUT

If your audience is a group that is unfamiliar to you, perhaps do some research and get to know them a little first. If you are designing a production for very young children, then it might be a good idea to visit the class that will be coming, or spend some time with younger family members and talk to them about what they are interested in and stories they like.

Role-play your audience participation with members of your group, or possibly other students not connected with your production, to give you experience of managing challenging behaviour. If you practise with very challenging situations, the reality will seem very easy and straightforward. For example, have a very shy and embarrassed volunteer, someone who is a total show off, someone aggressive and so on.

 VIDEO LINK

Watch the video about connecting with an audience at www.brightredbooks.net/N5Drama

 ONLINE

There is a useful article about audience participation from the *Guardian* at www.brightredbooks.net/N5Drama

DON'T FORGET

Make sure that you identify your audience in your support log and outline how you took them into consideration in your production.

 ONLINE TEST

Test yourself on this topic at www.brightredbooks.net/N5Drama

DRAMA SKILLS

SELECTING STIMULI

DRAMA SKILLS: OVERVIEW

For the drama skills elements of the course you will be required to develop your own production from a stimulus which may include text. You might have the opportunity to write your own script, take a production role or direct, so there are many options to consider. There are a number of skills you should aim to develop.

USING A RANGE OF DRAMA SKILLS

Use a range of drama skills by:

1.1 **Responding to a range of stimuli, including text, to develop ideas for drama** – you will be creative in your response to a stimulus, generating, combining and selecting appropriate ideas and working with others.

1.2 **Developing a range of drama skills to communicate ideas** – you will do this by experimenting with ideas through games, improvisation and rehearsals and by trying out different techniques and conventions to understand how they contribute to mood, atmosphere and audience reaction.

1.3 **Applying a range of drama skills to communicate ideas** – you will put into practice what you learn by experimenting and developing your ideas in a production that communicates an idea to an audience effectively.

1.4 **Evaluating your own work and that of others** – you will be able to critically evaluate your work and give an opinion about what you do well and what might need further development.

CONTRIBUTING TO THE DRAMA PROCESS

Contribute to the drama process by:

2.1 **Researching, planning and devising drama** – you should develop research skills and be able to discuss the social and cultural background to a production. You will contribute to planning a production that might involve writing a script.

2.2 **Using a range of acting skills in order to portray character** – you must show an understanding of how to develop and communicate character to an audience. This will involve a range of skills, including voice and movement techniques.

2.3 **Exploring form, genre, structure and style** – in developing drama you will have the opportunity to experiment with form, genre, structure and style and to choose the appropriate techniques for your form. This will involve a consideration of who your audience is and the best way to communicate with them.

2.4 **Evaluating your own work and that of others** – this will involve you thinking carefully about how effective your work is and where it can be improved.

Your teacher will assess your work as you progress through the course and you must provide evidence that you have responded to a range of stimuli (including text), used a range of skills in acting and have evaluated your own work and that of others. This evidence should be recorded in your **support log**.

DON'T FORGET

Depending on the scale of your production, it could take anywhere from six to 12 weeks to develop, experiment, rehearse and perform your production.

SELECTING A STIMULUS: AN OVERVIEW

Absolutely anything can be a stimulus for drama. All objects, songs, photographs and paintings have a story behind them and it can be great fun imagining what this could be. During your course, some decisions about the stimulus and other aspects of your production might be made for you, but it is useful to look at the options available and the possibilities for responding to them anyway.

Let's now have a look at ideas for stimuli!

The liar, the witch and the wardrobe

Amazing man has lived 16 times

Murderer says detective ruined his reputation

NEWSPAPERS

Look at newspapers for topical stories and themes. The internet is a great source for these, but any newspaper you can get hold of will have something you can work with. Look at the headline and avoid reading the story to allow your imagination complete freedom to interpret what the story might be about.

PHOTOGRAPHS

Old photographs can be really interesting and they are very easy to find online. You could start by recreating the photograph as a **tableau,** then bring it to life or do some **thought tracking** with the characters. Explore what could have been happening in that moment that the photograph was taken. Were all the characters happy to be there? Is there some underlying tension between the characters? What could that be?

ART

Art can also be really interesting as a stimulus, and you could choose anything from sculpture to paintings. You could choose a figurative/representational painting or something more **abstract**. Abstract might seem more difficult to use as a stimulus at first but an abstract painting, for example, can mean many things to many people and it will stimulate interesting discussions about how each member of the group interprets it. Start by discussing atmosphere and mood and see where it takes you.

OBJECTS

Even the most mundane objects could have a fascinating story behind them. Something that has been discarded in the street could have a fantastic and adventurous back story to explain how it came to be there – for example, a shoe, a lottery ticket, nutcrackers, a key, a diary or an item of clothing. Could it have been discarded, lost or stolen? Why? Did the person who stole it need it? Why? And so on.

A PIECE OF MUSIC OR A SONG

Music can be very evocative and is therefore a great stimulus for creative drama. You can have fun responding to music through movement first, and see where it leads. Music is also rooted in time and culture, so there are endless social and cultural elements that can be researched and incorporated into the drama.

A POEM

Poetry, like music, can also be wonderfully evocative. Some poems tell a story, which could be an excellent starting point for you to flesh it out further and explore some of the images it presents. Others can be more abstract and deal with a mood or emotion.

Try reading the poem aloud first and then consider what performance techniques or elements could bring it to life for an audience. Some ideas to get you started are *Originally* – Carol Ann Duffy, *We Refugees* – Benjamin Zephaniah and *Fundamentalism* – Naomi Shihab Nye.

VIDEO LINK

Watch a video of a simple response to a poem as a stimulus at www.brightredbooks.net/N5Drama

DON'T FORGET

You can keep a record in your support log of ideas for stimuli. Anything you come across that seems interesting or generates ideas could be useful one day.

ONLINE TEST

Test your knowledge about selecting stimuli online at www.brightredbooks.net/N5Drama

THINGS TO DO AND THINK ABOUT

Create a stimuli box which contains a variety of each type of stimulus. Practise responding to a stimulus by having one person pull something out of the box which the group then has to respond to. You could start by just telling the story either individually or collectively and then try to act it out.

RESPONDING TO A STIMULUS

CREATING YOUR RESPONSE

Once you have chosen or are presented with a stimulus, you will need to start creating your response to it. This might appear more daunting than responding to a text where you already have the words that the characters will say, which give you clues and a great deal of direction as to where to take the performance. However, with other types of stimuli you have more creative freedom in designing your response. This can be exciting but it might also seem confusing as you could take your response in any number of directions. It might help to go through the steps outlined here to give some shape and direction to the process of generating ideas. Then you can have fun trying out the different ideas that arise from this.

There are many ways to structure and organise a creative process and many theories about the best way to do this. You can adapt the following example for your own purposes. It might help to follow the steps in order, but you could also find that if you encounter problems you need to go back and revisit some of the steps to work through them. You could also discover that it helps to do two steps at the same time – for example, **Experimentation** and **Evaluation** might happen simultaneously. As you try out ideas, you might find that something doesn't work and discard it straightaway.

THE CREATIVE PROCESS

1. GENERATE IDEAS

Spend some time generating as many ideas that relate to the stimulus as you can. Start off simply with words, hunches and feelings: gather lots of suggestions and make notes as you go. Keep in mind the 'when, where, why, what' questions from the section on responding to a text (pp 88–89). Doing some research on the theme might help get you started. The next section (pp 14–15) has many suggestions on how to generate ideas.

2. EXPERIMENT

Start to play with the ideas. Select a few that seem to have potential or that all members of the group are inspired by, and begin to develop them a little further and experiment with them in different ways. The section on experimenting with ideas (pp 20–21) should help you with this.

3. EVALUATION/CRITICAL REVIEW

This is where you review your work and learn from it. The aim is to decide which is the most fertile idea, or whether several ideas should be combined. Discuss with your partner or group how things seemed and felt when you tried them. You could perhaps involve an audience or classmates in another group for **constructive criticism**. Weigh up the pros and cons and try to identify what is good and what is more challenging with each idea.

4. SELECTION OF AN IDEA

Your evaluation will hopefully help you to decide which ideas to work on further. The group must come to some kind of consensus. This might happen easily, or it might be more tricky. Consider all the important elements in this decision. What will appeal to your audience? Do you have the technical capabilities required? Are you confident that you can achieve your aim? It is important to be ambitious but also realistic.

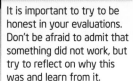

DON'T FORGET

It is important to try to be honest in your evaluations. Don't be afraid to admit that something did not work, but try to reflect on why this was and learn from it.

contd

5. DEVELOPMENT

Once you have selected your best idea, you can begin to develop it into a production, working in rehearsals on your narrative, characterisation, style and conventions. The following chapters will help you with this. An important tip is to know when to stop – don't overwork it. Give yourself enough time to have periods where you can pause and give it time to develop. Sometimes you need a break and time to reflect, particularly if you encounter problems.

 THINGS TO DO AND THINK ABOUT

Have a schedule. Decide how long you will spend generating ideas and when you will move onto the next stage. Without this, you could go on generating ideas forever.

Write it/draw it. It sometimes helps to see things visually so you can see that you are making progress. Write down all the initial ideas on big sheets of paper stuck to the wall. As you start to narrow down and refine the ideas, add more sheets to make notes on the developments as you go. Keep all the sheets as you might need to refer back to them, and they can form part of your support log.

Take time out. Whenever things seem to be stuck or get too frustrating, take time out. Creating can be a difficult process, but it cannot be forced. Sometimes ideas come when you are focusing on something else. If you have time, play a game for ten minutes or do something physical. If you leave it alone for a while, it will probably be easier when you come back to it. If time is tight, ask your teacher for help as another perspective can also be very useful.

DON'T FORGET

Record the whole process in your support log, particularly the reasons for your decisions.

 ONLINE TEST

Test your knowledge about responding to stimuli online at www.brightredbooks.net/N5Drama

 ONLINE

For an extra activity in responding to stimuli, head to www.brightredbooks.net/N5Drama

GENERATING IDEAS

Whether you are working with a text or with another stimulus, you will need to begin by generating ideas for your dramatic response. There are many different methods of generating ideas. If you try out the following suggestions, you should end up with a variety of ideas to choose from. Creativity is all-important in this process, and this happens best when you just let the ideas flow. A safe and non-intimidating environment in which all members of the group feel confident about contributing their ideas is also essential. So, before you begin, agree on a few ground rules to facilitate the discussion.

TOP TIPS FOR DISCUSSION GUIDELINES

- Keep everything positive. All ideas and suggestions are equal and important at this stage. The aim at first is to collect as many ideas as possible, so there is no point in discarding ideas now.

- Make a note of all ideas without judging them. It is not fair to judge some ideas as noteworthy and others as not, so make a note of every suggestion. You can evaluate them later.

- People can contribute if they want to. No-one should be forced to speak. Some people are more confident about offering ideas in this format than others, and some need more time to think. If people feel intimidated, they are unlikely to come up with a brilliant idea.

WARM-UPS

Start with some creative warm-ups. These simple and fun games get everyone in the right frame of mind to let the ideas flow. Games that involve some **improvisation** or making up stories on the spot are good starters.

FORTUNATELY, UNFORTUNATELY

Everyone sits in a circle and one person will start telling a story. They must tell one line of the story beginning with the word 'fortunately'. The next person then continues the story with the next line beginning with the word 'unfortunately' – and so on around the circle.

THE LETTER

This is a quick improvisation game which involves having to respond to an unknown stimulus. Everyone sits in a circle. One person goes into the middle of the circle and begins an improvisation. They can be doing anything they like to start off with – for example, making a cup of tea, waiting at a bus stop in the rain or sleeping. Another person then enters the improvisation carrying a letter. It is up to the second person what is in the letter, but they must communicate it to the first person, who must then respond appropriately. Let the improvisation run for a couple of minutes and then give others a turn.

DIE BY

This is a fun improvisation game that really tests creativity. Three people begin an improvisation with a situation that they have chosen or that someone else has chosen for them. Something fairly mundane like shopping in the supermarket or watching a film at the cinema works well. After a minute or so another member of the group shouts 'die by ...' followed by a bizarre method of death. For example, 'die by octopus' or 'die by banana'. It is best if the method of death has nothing to do with the improvisation in progress. The actors must then seamlessly continue the improvisation but work in at least one of the characters dying by the chosen method.

CREATIVE ACTIVITIES

After a short warm-up, start to generate some ideas. Hopefully, everyone will be feeling creative.

- Begin with word association, and just list all the related words that come to mind when you think of your text or stimulus.

- Mind maps and spider diagrams can be really useful ways of recording ideas and making connections. You don't need to do this with a pen and paper, although it can sometimes be the easiest way. Have a look at the electronic tools available to see if they help. There are many apps and websites that offer a way to create digital mind maps and make connections between related ideas.

- Play storytelling games with your group using the text or stimulus. Without giving it too much thought, pick a character or an incident from the play or look at the stimulus and just start telling a story either individually or together. The chances are that it won't all work, but some good ideas will probably come out of it.

- Collect information about the stimulus onto a mood board. This could be an actual pinboard or a digital one. Collect newspaper articles, film, music and images – everything that you can find that relates to it –and pin it up to create a kind of collage. This will create a visual picture of everyone's thoughts about the stimulus. Stand back and look at it occasionally to see the overall impression it creates.

- Get up and start improvising. For example, if your stimulus is a prop, try taking turns to improvise scenes where you use it in different ways. If you are using a text, pick a scene and role-play it in different styles such as film noir or action hero, or as if it's a game show. You could film your improvisations and watch them back, taking notes of what worked well.

- Do some research first if the ideas don't start flowing straightaway. Some stimuli are easier to respond to than others, so if you feel like you don't know enough about it spend some time researching to get you started.

- Sketch your ideas. Not everyone works best with words – some people are more comfortable with drawing ideas. You could draw storyboards like comic strips.

- Likewise, you can record your ideas on a sound recorder. Discussions can be recorded and listened to later to draw out the important ideas. You can also collect sounds. Sounds that relate to your text or stimulus can inspire ideas. If your stimulus is a photograph on a beach, recording the sounds of the sea, wind and seagulls might be a great place to start.

THINGS TO DO AND THINK ABOUT

Pick a stimulus from a hat and play a word association game. Pass the stimulus round the circle and each person should say the first word that occurs to them when they look at it. Make a note of all the words. Look at the list of words and make connections between those that seem to be linked.

If you are working with an image or photograph, stick it in the middle of a large sheet of paper and stick the paper to the wall. Leave it there for a week so anyone can add their impressions or ideas to it. You can then have a look at it and discuss together what has appeared on the paper.

Discuss your text or stimulus with others not studying drama. Sometimes you are too close to be able to see the wood for the trees. Someone not involved could make connections or have ideas that you haven't considered.

RESEARCH SKILLS

THE IMPORTANCE OF RESEARCH

Whatever stimulus you are responding to, you need to do some research around your theme. In your final performance assessment, your support log must demonstrate that you have an awareness of the social and cultural background to your piece, so it is vital to practise your research skills. Also, if you are struggling for ideas, doing some research on the theme first can help to generate them.

Effective research takes organisation. There is a wealth of information out there, so it is easy to get overwhelmed and lose focus. Be clear about what you want to find out, and keep a record of your results. You will discover connections that you hadn't considered. Remember, however, that although it is fine to follow a new tangent, always keep your aim in mind.

Everyone has their own preferred research methods, but here are some tips to start you off.

SOURCES OF INFORMATION

INTERNET

The internet is a huge source of information. However, be discerning and check your sources. Remember that anyone can contribute to websites like Wikipedia and that the information might not always be accurate. Double-check any facts you use by ensuring that several sources agree that it is true.

Don't rely too heavily on the internet, as there are still many alternative ways to research.

TALK TO PEOPLE

There's no substitute for a first-hand story. Always remember that you are getting one person's perspective on the story, but this is often what can make a story interesting. Pay attention to the way a story is told too, as this can be a great source of ideas for characterisation. Being able to ask questions of someone who has actually experienced what you are researching is invaluable.

PHOTOGRAPHY/IMAGES

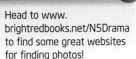

ONLINE

Head to www. brightredbooks.net/N5Drama to find some great websites for finding photos!

If you are using the internet, remember to search for images that relate to your theme. You could end up with some unexpected connections, or get a feel for a place through the images. You can also use photography to document a place. For example, if your drama is going to be set in your local area, try going out with a camera and documenting what you see. This will give you a different perspective on an area you probably no longer notice.

RECORD VOICES AND SOUNDS

Remember that voice and sound is an important part of drama, so don't discount researching how people might speak or what places might sound like. You could end up being inspired by the ambient sounds of a shopping centre, or the silence of a school at night.

FIRST-HAND EXPERIENCE

If there is an opportunity to get first-hand experience of something, then take it. For example, there is no harm in asking if you can visit a newspaper office or a bakery if you want to see what it is like to work there. Obviously, whatever you do has to be safe and legal!

ONLINE

Head to www. brightredbooks.net/N5Drama and follow the link to the Scottish Screen Archive to check it out!

FILM

YouTube is a great source for film clips and videos of theatre productions. Organisations like the Scottish Screen Archive have an archive of historical films about many subjects that you can watch online.

contd

BOOKS

Not all information is available online. Libraries are still an excellent source of information, particularly for historical texts and old newspapers and magazines. Remember that if a book you need is not available in your local library, they can order it from another library for you.

This list is not exhaustive. There will be many other sources of information available to you, so be creative and curious in your search.

TOP TIPS FOR RESEARCH

- Be organised – have questions you want to find the answers to.
- Be discerning – some information online can be misleading or incorrect.
- Make connections – follow new leads but keep your aim in mind.
- Be creative – use different types of information source.

MAKING NOTES

During your research, it is essential that you keep notes of what you find out. This can be done in any number of ways. You can write it all down in a notebook or perhaps keep a scrap book for ideas that you can stick things into.

Alternatively, you could use one of the many electronic methods for storing notes. Web-based applications and websites like Delicious or Google Keep are useful. You could also use a Glow eportfolio blog to collect all your ideas. The advantage of using a digital method is that you can bookmark music, films, images and text all in one place.

Think about what would suit your needs best. When and where will you need to access your support log? What format will enable you to do this? There is more help and information about this in the support log sections (pp 64–65 and 90–91).

THINGS TO DO AND THINK ABOUT

Once you have a broad idea or theme for your drama, try to come up with a list of five questions you think you would need to find the answers to.

Allocate a question or two to each group member to research and ask them to use any of the methods listed above.

In your next session, each group member should present their research findings to the rest of the group, so you can share the information.

DON'T FORGET

Be flexible in your search and think laterally. If you get no results searching for what you are looking for, use a related word or idea.

DON'T FORGET

Every time you find something useful or follow a link, make a note of where it is. This is important because you need to list your research sources in your support log. It is also very frustrating when you know that you have seen something somewhere, but you can't find it again.

ONLINE TEST

Head to www. brightredbooks.net/N5Drama and take the test on research skills.

SOCIAL AND CULTURAL INFLUENCES

As mentioned in the previous chapter, it is important that you can demonstrate an awareness of the **social and cultural influences** on your drama work. All plays or devised performances are a product of their particular time and place, so the social and cultural influences of the time will have affected the writing. Even if it is not immediately obvious, we can identify these influences in the way characters behave, speak and relate to one another.

During your research, you will be guided by the main theme you decide to focus on, but it is useful to keep in mind other areas that could inform your drama. Try giving the following issues some thought in your research.

THEMES TO RESEARCH

GENDER

A production of Sophocles' *Antigone*

Attitudes and beliefs about gender roles have changed throughout history and differ according to specific cultures. Think about the time period and culture of your setting. Are there certain things you need to consider about gender – for example, the feminist movement of the 60s and 70s? How would women behave and how would this been seen by the rest of society? In Sophocles' *Antigone*, for example, which was written around 441 BC and is set in Thebes, you would need to think about the way in which the Greek society of the time viewed women, and how Antigone's behaviour fits in with that.

RACE

Attitudes towards racial difference and issues such as mixed-race relationships have changed and this might require consideration in your drama. Researching people's personal stories and their feelings about race along with the general attitudes of the time will help if you are portraying a character in this position. For example, the character of Jo in *A Taste of Honey* by Shelagh Delaney lives in Salford in North West England in the 1950s, when attitudes towards mixed-race relationships were very different to today.

A production of *A Taste of Honey* by Shelagh Delaney

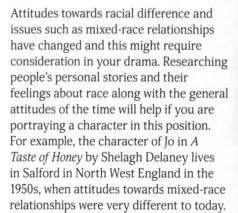
A production of Oscar Wilde's *The Importance of being Ernest*

SEXUALITY

Again, attitudes have changed towards sexuality. It is not really that long ago that homosexuality was illegal in the UK, and it is still discriminated against in many parts of the world. Some plays – like *Cloud Nine* by Caryl Churchill – deal with this directly, but others – such as Oscar Wilde's *The Importance of being Ernest*, written in 1895 – have more of an undercurrent or subtext because of the time in which they are set.

contd

ACTIVITY

If you are interested in these issues, research one of the plays mentioned and find out about the political and social themes of the time. This could be a useful starting point for your own work.

CUSTOMS

If your production is to be set in a country or culture you are not familiar with, research some of the customs of the place and time. Likewise, think about diversity in your production. To reflect a diverse society, you will probably have to research the customs of other cultures living in the UK. Quite often when people are displaced from their homeland, customs can become even more important to them because it's a link to their original culture.

RELIGION

Religion can have many parallels with racial issues and it also incorporates customs and rituals that you might be unfamiliar with. Understanding the beliefs and the significance of religion to a society could be important if you are dealing with themes of bullying, sectarianism, terrorism, difference and even football.

EDUCATION

When researching a character, it might be useful to consider the kind of education that character has received and how this might have affected their view of the world, ambitions and possibly the way they speak.

WAR/TERRORISM

Even if you are not focusing on war or terrorism as a theme, it can have a significant effect on a society. For example the ongoing **war on terror** creates significant paranoia in society today and heightens racial and religious tension in many places. In the UK, some ethnic or religious groups can experience more harassment after a terrorist attack, which can result in bullying and suspicion in school and on the street.

HEALTH

Standards in health care and hygiene have changed over time, so consider this in your production – particularly if it is historical. Think about the beliefs about cures for the Black Death, and the kind of illnesses that people regularly suffered from. In medieval times, for example, there was no knowledge of germs: disease was thought to be a punishment from God, bad luck or influenced by the stars.

THINGS TO DO AND THINK ABOUT

Thinking about your script or stimulus, decide when and where you will set your drama. Do a search online for a newspaper from that time and place. (Google News has a reasonable archive of historical newspapers.) The newspaper will give you a good indication of the important issues of the day, which you can then research further.

Allocate an appropriate issue to each group member. Each person should research the issue and return to the group with three ways in which it might affect the drama.

If you are using a historical play, read through it and list all the themes and issues that are relevant to a modern audience such as jealousy, bullying, discrimination and lust for power.

DON'T FORGET

This list is not exhaustive: there are many other issues you can consider such as politics, technology, fashions and popular culture.

DON'T FORGET

You might decide to update an older play and concentrate on the themes that are still relevant today.

ONLINE

Head to www. brightredbooks.net/ N5Drama for a useful resource from the BBC that uses Macbeth as an example of how to research themes.

ONLINE TEST

Test yourself on your knowledge of researching social and cultural influences at www.brightredbooks.net/ N5Drama

EXPERIMENTING WITH IDEAS

TRY IT OUT

Once you have generated a good bank of ideas that relate to your stimulus or text, it is time to start experimenting. When developing drama, it is important to remember that it is an expressive art. Although thinking and discussing are good, you should spend a good deal of your time playing, performing and experimenting to see how things work. Sometimes what seems like a brilliant idea in theory will turn out not to work in practice, and the most unlikely idea will be really effective when performed. There is only one way to find this out. Get up and do it!

Through the process of experimentation, you will begin to develop and refine the ideas further. You can combine ideas and try them out in different ways. Keep an open mind and just see what happens: making unexpected connections is how you will discover something brilliant and original.

ONLINE

Head to www. brightredbooks.net/N5Drama for some great ideas for hotseat questions.

CHARACTER DEVELOPMENT

If you already have some characters in mind for your performance, try them out at this point.

WEAR MASKS

Use masks to develop how characters might move. Using a neutral mask will encourage you to focus on body language, because you cannot use voice or facial expression to communicate. Experiment with different walks, postures and gestures for your characters.

GET IN THE HOT-SEAT

Identify potential characters by putting different actors on the **hot-seat** and interviewing them in role. This will help to develop the characters' backgrounds and personalities and you might discover that a member of the group is great at performing a particular character.

PLAY GAMES

Try some relationship and **status** games. Improvise various scenarios with characters, changing their relationships and status. For example, if you have a teenage character and an older person, try putting them in a situation where they have different types of relationship. You could try a grandparent and grandchild, employer and employee, patient and carer, teacher and student or a criminal and victim. Play around and see what happens when power is shifted between them.

THEMES

To experiment with the themes you are considering, you could role-play a television programme about it. For example, if you are considering bullying as a theme, imagine that you are making a television documentary about the effects of bullying. Members of the group can take on different characters such as victim, bully, witness, teacher or police officer, and can be interviewed about what happens and how they feel about it.

If you are exploring fame, you could have a celebrity, their family members, fans, paparazzi and so on.

PLOT

Develop the plot by experimenting with telling the story in different ways. If you have several ideas, try them out with the instant performance game. One person takes on the role of **narrator** and the rest of the group take on characters in the story. The narrator then tells the story and the actors perform the story in real time. The narrator can add bits into the story as it occurs to them and the performers must respond accordingly. You can take it in turns to be the narrator and refine the story as you go, or change it completely. This is great fun and it also helps you to picture how the story might work in action.

BIG PITCH

If you are trying to develop a production concept, imagine that you have to pitch your idea to a funder. They have the money and will only give it to you to put on your show if you sell the idea to them. You have to persuade them that your show will work and that people will want to come and see it. This will help you to think through the reasons for your choices and whether or not the production really will work. You could pitch your idea to a panel of students from another group, or to your teacher. If they refuse to fund you, ask them for feedback to help you understand their decision, and what you can do to improve your pitch.

Using some of the ideas in the chapter on rehearsal techniques (pp 50–51) will also help you to develop your ideas further.

DON'T FORGET

Follow leads that appear to work well. If something clicks and you want to develop it further, then go for it.

DON'T FORGET

While you are experimenting, identify problems and possible solutions in your support log.

THINGS TO DO AND THINK ABOUT

Put all your story ideas on individual pieces of paper and put them in a hat. Then put a selection of different styles and genres of drama in a different hat. Pick one piece of paper from each hat and improvise a scene in that style. You might end up having to improvise a story about teenage pregnancy through **mime** or exploring the theme of homelessness in the style of a **farce**.

Do the same for possible characters. Put all the ideas for the characters you might like to use in one hat and a selection of possible scenarios in another. Pick one from each and improvise. This time you might end up being an old lady in a nightclub or an Elizabethan nobleman involved in a robbery!

Consider the style of drama that will suit what you are trying to say to the audience.

ONLINE TEST

Test yourself on experimenting with ideas at www.brightredbooks.net/N5Drama

DRAMA FORM

Drama **form** is a very difficult thing to define. You will find that the terms **form**, **genre** and **style** all seem interchangeable when discussing drama and that the definitions overlap depending on what you are reading or whom you are talking to. You will even find that some forms also feature in a list of **theatre conventions**. Be aware that most of the forms described here could also be on a list of **drama styles** or **genres**, so don't be too rigid with these definitions.

Generally speaking, drama or theatre form is the **shape** of the drama. Certain productions use particular **conventions** and **techniques** that give it a certain character and it falls into a category because of this. Categorising drama in this way helps an audience to read a performance as they understand the **conventions** used and have certain expectations of the form. It has nothing to do with content: it's more about the **structure** and shape of the narrative rather than what happens or how it's performed.

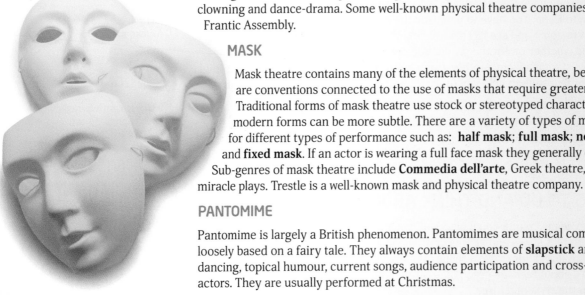

VIDEO LINK

Check out the clips 'DV8: The Cost of Living' and 'Frantic Assembly Ignition 2009 Bed Scene' at www. brightredbooks.net/N5Drama

COMMON FORMS

PLAY – SCRIPTED OR IMPROVISED

At the most basic level of form a play or a performance can be either scripted or improvised. There may be elements of both or it may be a performance based on **rehearsed improvisation**.

PHYSICAL THEATRE

Physical theatre emphasises physical movement as a form of expression. Some physical theatre productions also use speech or song, but the physical movement is the principle mode of expression.

These productions are usually devised rather than scripted. They often combine music, dance, mime and visual art and encourage either audience participation or performers coming into the audience space. Sub-genres of physical theatre can be mime, circus, clowning and dance-drama. Some well-known physical theatre companies are DV8 and Frantic Assembly.

MASK

Mask theatre contains many of the elements of physical theatre, because there are conventions connected to the use of masks that require greater physicality. Traditional forms of mask theatre use stock or stereotyped characters but more modern forms can be more subtle. There are a variety of types of mask that allow for different types of performance such as: **half mask**; **full mask**; **neutral mask** and **fixed mask**. If an actor is wearing a full face mask they generally don't speak. Sub-genres of mask theatre include **Commedia dell'arte**, Greek theatre, mystery and miracle plays. Trestle is a well-known mask and physical theatre company.

PANTOMIME

Pantomime is largely a British phenomenon. Pantomimes are musical comedies, usually loosely based on a fairy tale. They always contain elements of **slapstick** and farce, dancing, topical humour, current songs, audience participation and cross-dressing actors. They are usually performed at Christmas.

DANCE-DRAMA

This is a sub-genre of physical theatre and in western theatre this is strongly influenced by contemporary dance. It differs from physical theatre in that the action is mainly set to music and the story is told through dance. There are many different forms of dance drama with well-known examples from Japan, India and Indonesia.

contd

MIME

Mime is the performance of a story without the use of speech. It is closely related to mask and physical theatre, because the emphasis is on physical movement for expression. Famous practitioners include Charlie Chaplin, Rowan Atkinson and Marcel Marceau.

MONOLOGUE

This is a **device** found in various forms of drama and is included in the techniques and conventions chapter (pp 36–37). It can, however, also be a genre of drama in the form of **monologue** plays or one-person shows.

PUPPET

This is an extremely old form of theatre that involves storytelling through the use of varying types of puppet. Chinese Shadow Theatre and Japanese Bunraku puppet theatre are well-known examples. Many modern productions such as *War Horse* and the National Theatre of Scotland's 2012 production of *A Christmas Carol* use a mixture of puppets and live action very successfully.

DON'T FORGET

These are broad categories and many productions will not fit easily into only one category. Many use elements of several forms.

VIDEO LINK

There are clips of inspiring productions at www. brightredbooks.net/N5Drama and a fascinating talk about how the horses in *War Horse* were made.

DON'T FORGET

The form that you choose for your own production will be influenced in large part either by the text you are using or by your audience and what will appeal to them.

ONLINE TEST

Take the 'Drama Form' test at www.brightredbooks.net/N5Drama

THINGS TO DO AND THINK ABOUT

Experiment by performing well-known stories in different forms. You could try *Little Red Riding Hood* as physical theatre, *Jack and the Beanstalk* as mask theatre or even *Romeo and Juliet* as pantomime (although you might have to change the ending).

Try mixing up forms and genres. Experiment with a tragic mime or a masked melodrama. This can be good fun, and helps you to learn the **conventions** and **techniques** involved.

DRAMA GENRE

In the previous section (pp 22–23) we looked at how **form** and genre overlap considerably and how people often use the terms interchangeably when discussing theatre and drama. We also looked at some common and broad theatre forms.

In this section, we're going to look at some common **genres** in drama. This list is not exhaustive, and you will come across many more genres that are not mentioned here.

COMMON GENRES

COMEDY

There are many different types of comedy, but ultimately it should be funny and make the audience laugh. Within this genre, there are sub-genres like **parody**, **satire**, **slapstick**, **farce**, **comedy of manners** and **romantic comedy**.

Generally – unless it's a black comedy – a comedy has a happy ending with good characters rewarded and bad punished. Ridiculous things can happen and characters are often stereotypes such as a greedy lawyer or a stupid model. Comedies often use mistaken identities and verbal humour such as puns, malapropisms and exaggeration. Examples are *The Importance of Being Ernest* by Oscar Wilde and *Noises Off* by Michael Frayn.

TRAGEDY

Tragedy is a classical genre of drama that originated with the ancient Greeks. It focuses on themes of human suffering and man's place in the universe. There is usually a conflict between the main character and some kind of superior force like destiny or the gods. Typically, the main character has a tragic flaw and brings about his own downfall, which arouses the audience's fear and pity. It is not essential for the main character to die in a tragedy, but Shakespeare's normally do. There are many sub-genres of tragedy such as Greek tragedy, Roman tragedy, Elizabethan tragedy and Modern tragedy. Famous examples of tragedies include Shakespeare's *King Lear* and *Romeo and Juliet*.

MELODRAMA

Melodramas are over the top! They exaggerate plot and characters to appeal to the emotions. They are characterised by intense action, some kind of terrible disaster and intense emotion. They were popular in Victorian times when they included the use of signature music to signify a particular emotion or character. They have simple, exaggerated, good-and-evil stories with happy endings. The plot and action are more important than the (typically) one-dimensional characters. Traditionally, there was a hero, a heroine (who has to be rescued), a villain, a villain's accomplice, a faithful servant and a flirty and loyal maidservant. Quite a few modern action and romantic comedy films use this formula with great success.

HISTORICAL

These plays are based on historical events and famous people from history. They don't necessarily stick to the facts and will often be fictionalised. *Saint Joan* by George Bernard Shaw is an example of this genre.

KITCHEN-SINK/SOCIAL REALISM

Kitchen-sink drama deals with the real-life situations of the working class, and was developed in the 1950s and 60s. John Osbourne's *Look Back in Anger* is a famous example of this.

TRAGICOMEDY

Tragicomedy combines elements of both comedy and tragedy. It can often be a serious play with a happy ending or a funny play with a sad ending. These plays are sometimes called romances, like Shakespeare's *The Merchant of Venice*.

DOCU-DRAMA OR DOCUMENTARY THEATRE

These productions are dramatised re-enactments of real events and they attempt to stick as closely to the facts as possible. They often include sound recordings from the event or film clips of actual events and places. The National Theatre of Scotland's *Black Watch* is a powerful example of this genre.

VIDEO LINK

The National Theatre has some informative films about Commedia dell'arte – check them out at www. brightredbooks.net/N5Drama

THEATRE FOR DEVELOPMENT

This is a form of **participatory theatre** developed for the purpose of international development. It's a way of encouraging the audience or participants to identify and solve their own problems, empowering communities to make sustainable changes.

COMMEDIA DELL'ARTE

Commedia dell'arte is a hugely influential form of fifteenth-century Italian street theatre. Troupes of performers would tour the country, improvising scenes based on masked stock characters that the audience would immediately recognise. Many practitioners of physical and mask theatre forms will cite Commedia dell'arte as an influence on their work.

THEATRE IN EDUCATION

Theatre in Education is a form designed specifically to encourage learning and debate through theatre and drama. It is often performed in schools, and involves a high level of audience participation. This form uses mobile and minimal sets.

THINGS TO DO AND THINK ABOUT

To help you learn more about some of these drama genres, each member of your group could choose one of the genres that they know very little about, research it and give a presentation about it to the rest of the group.

Have some fun with the genre game. You will need two large cubes for this. On the sides of one cube stick the names of famous stories. They could be fairy tales, Shakespeare plays or famous movies. On the sides of the other cube stick a variety of drama genres. You now have two dice. Split the group into pairs or threes and each group takes it in turns to roll the dice and improvise the story in the appropriate genre. This is usually very funny!

Think about collecting and categorising productions you have seen. Perhaps this could be a display on the wall in your classroom or studio. Each time someone sees a production you can discuss it and try to fit it into the correct form or genre. This will result in some good discussions about form and genre and develop into a useful display.

DON'T FORGET

You will almost certainly come across many more genres than the ones mentioned here.

ONLINE TEST

Take the 'Drama Form' test at www.brightredbooks.net/ N5Drama

DRAMA STYLE

The definition of **style** differs from form and genre slightly, but there is considerable overlap and you will find many of the following terms on lists of drama forms and vice versa.

The **style** of drama focuses more on the **way** in which the story is told – this includes the way it is acted and the contribution made to the drama by production techniques such as lighting, costume, make-up and sound. Quite often these styles have parallels in literature, art and architecture.

EXAMPLES OF STYLE

NATURALISM

This was a nineteenth and early twentieth-century movement in theatre, which aimed to create a perfect illusion of reality. These productions created realistic settings and stories in an effort to expose the harsh realities of life, often addressing issues such as sexuality, poverty and racism. The illusion was all-important, so devices such as narrators or tableaux were dismissed as unsuitable because they would shatter that illusion. The audience was supposed to be absorbed within the fiction as if they were watching real life happening in front of them. An example of this style can be seen in *A Doll's House* by Henrik Ibsen.

SOCIAL REALISM

This was a movement in art, television, literature and film, and in Britain it was called 'Kitchen-Sink' drama because of its focus on domestic settings. This style of theatre explored themes around social inequality and political controversy to draw attention to the conditions of the working class and poor. The male heroes of these stories were often referred to as 'angry young men'. *A Taste of Honey* by Shelagh Delaney is an example of this style of play.

SURREALISM

Originating around the 1920s and heavily influenced by Freud's psychoanalysis, **surrealist** theatre was an attempt to find the truth or core of the self – uninhibited by the conscious mind – to overcome the traditions and culture that oppress freedom. To portray this, surrealist playwrights experimented with writing whatever came to mind without the conscious mind trying to make sense of it. Plays would mix dreams and reality and present unexpected and apparently irrational connections.

THEATRE OF THE ABSURD

Theatre of the Absurd was influenced by surrealism and shares the same characteristics of lack of clear cause, effect or logic. At its core is a belief that human existence has no meaning or purpose, and this can result in unexplained settings and meaningless tasks that make the audience feel slightly uncomfortable. This style often uses comedy in the form of nonsense speech or ridiculous connections, but many of the characters also appear quite tragic. There may be no resolution in an absurd story, as they often don't follow a traditional story arc structure. Samuel Beckett's *Waiting for Godot* is a famous example of this style, with Harold Pinter and Jean Genet also well-known absurdists.

EXPRESSIONISM

Expressionism is an early twentieth-century style of drama that originated in Germany. The characteristics of expressionism include simplified characters, choral effects, declamatory dialogue, intensity, fragmented action, spiritual awakenings and suffering and struggles against established authority and the ruling class – often in the form of a father figure. In terms of production, it uses very stark sets, which are angled and distorted, stark lighting and the use of spotlights.

contd

MODERNISM

Modernism is a difficult and slippery term to define. In terms of the theatre, it seems to have begun with naturalism, but it also incorporates elements of realism and is heavily influenced by symbolism. (See the techniques and conventions chapter (pp 36–37) for more information about the use of symbols.) It has become almost like an umbrella term for anyone trying something experimental and new. Playwrights and practitioners as diverse as Ibsen, Brecht, Beckett, and Artaud have all been categorised as modernist.

POSTMODERNISM

Postmodernism moves away from the idea that theatre represents some kind of truth, and focuses more on the creation of meaning by the audience. Each person will take their own meaning from the performance, so the performance presents questions rather than answers. Narratives are **non-linear**, fragmented and involve many stories being interwoven together, and often include multimedia techniques. The audience could be included in the performance, and improvisation is important: the experience is created anew each time and will never be the same again.

SITE-SPECIFIC THEATRE

Site-specific theatre is a form designed for places not originally intended for theatrical performance. For example, an existing play such as *A Midsummer Night's Dream* might be performed in a forest, or a new play might be specifically devised for an unusual location like a shopping centre or a disused building.

PROMENADE THEATRE

In **promenade theatre** (sometimes called **immersive theatre**) the audience is expected to move around. There is often no formal stage and it can be in an unusual location. There are very few rules for this form as it deliberately challenges the audience's expectations. The action might take place spread across a city or you could be required to move from room to room. The audience members are quite often required to experience the drama alone or in small groups and could be expected to get involved in improvised sections. Punchdrunk is a theatre company well known for producing this type of theatre, with shows such as *The Hanged Man: A Hollywood Fable*.

DON'T FORGET

These descriptions are very general and many plays will include elements of more than one style of drama. Don't feel you have to stick rigidly to the description of the style.

A good example of postmodernism is the show *Fuerzabruta*

THINGS TO DO AND THINK ABOUT

Try this activity to practise **naturalistic** and melodramatic styles of acting. Stand in a circle so that everyone is visible. One person starts by performing a normal everyday action in a naturalistic way. The next person performs the same action but slightly exaggerates it. The next person exaggerates even more and so on until the last person performs it in a completely over-the-top way. Start again with a new action from a different person.

If you are aiming for a realistic style of acting, it helps to consider the **objectives** of your character. The objectives provide the **motivation** for everything your character does. Take one scene of your play and consider your character's objectives for each line, the movements they make, their overall objective for the scene and their super objective for their life. This will help you to understand your character's thoughts and desires and make for a more natural and believable performance.

ONLINE TEST

Take the 'Drama Style' test at www.brightredbooks.net/N5Drama

SELECTING IDEAS

If you have been successful in generating a number of ideas, your next challenge will be to select one or two to develop further. The chapter on experimenting with ideas (pp 20–21) will help with this. If you are still struggling to narrow the choice down, there are some suggestions in this section that you could try. But first, you need to think about the following things:

WHAT IS THE AIM?

Start with your aim or message. Do you want to inform or entertain – or both? What do you want to say to the audience? It might be that you want to say something about the importance of hope, or perhaps you want to take them on an emotional journey. Keep this in mind throughout the whole process, and make sure that everything you do contributes towards this aim.

DRAMATIC POTENTIAL

When you evaluate ideas, you are looking for their dramatic potential – for example, a rich theme or an issue that everyone can relate to, the potential for a satisfying ending, or a journey towards self-discovery, understanding or maturity.

By far the most important element for good drama, however, is **conflict**. As the playwright George Bernard Shaw pointed out, 'no conflict, no drama!'

Conflict in this sense does not necessarily mean a fight or a war (although they do occasionally play a part) but rather some kind of internal or external struggle to overcome something. The main character in a story is always involved in some kind of opposition to something. It is often said that there are four general categories of conflict, and that all stories are based on one of these.

Shakespeare's *Hamlet*

MAN VS HIMSELF

This is an internal conflict: a character fighting with an element of themselves such as shyness, addiction, inner demons and so on. *Hamlet* by Shakespeare is a good example of this kind of conflict. The central character struggles constantly with fear and self-doubt.

MAN VS NATURE

This is an external conflict that involves characters struggling with some element of nature, such as extreme weather or perhaps a vicious animal. *King Lear* by Shakespeare is an example of a play using this type of conflict.

MAN VS MAN

This is another type of external conflict where characters are in opposition to each other. Any story that involves a hero and a villain falls into this category. Fairy tales like *Snow White* and *Cinderella* are examples of this type of conflict.

contd

MAN VS SOCIETY

This involves any struggle against a political or social issue such as racism or sexism, where someone is fighting for a cause against the social norms of their time and place. Harper Lee's *To Kill a Mockingbird*, Henrik Ibsen's *A Doll's House* and Arthur Miller's *The Crucible* are examples of this kind of conflict.

A scene from *The Crucible*

The use of conflict in storytelling creates excitement for the audience, because it suggests that there is doubt about whether the struggle will be won.

It is common for a story to contain multiple conflicts, so don't feel that you have to choose just one. You might have a story that involves a 'man vs society' conflict, and an internal conflict.

PRACTICAL CONSIDERATIONS

You also need to think about the practical aspects of your idea. It is great to be inspired, creative and ambitious, but be realistic. Will your idea appeal to your audience? Have you got time to realise your vision in a satisfactory way? Do you have the resources or budget for elements such as costumes, special effects, props and set? Do you have the technical capabilities? Is your performance space appropriate and do you have the required sound and lighting equipment?

THINGS TO DO AND THINK ABOUT

Discard the ideas that you definitely don't like first. It's more difficult to choose from a big selection than from a small selection, so narrow your choice down to two or three ideas.

ONLINE

For a further look at dramatic conflicts, head to www.brightredbooks.net/N5Drama

DON'T FORGET

You are not making the decision alone. Good communication and compromise is key to this process.

ONLINE TEST

Test yourself on selecting ideas at www.brightredbooks.net/N5Drama

PRESENTING IDEAS

Once you have narrowed down your choice to two or three ideas, you might be asked to present them to the rest of the class or to another audience. This will help you to select the best idea to take forward into a production, and it will also help you if you are asked to present the results of your research or your work to an examiner.

GENERAL TIPS

- Be creative. Try to get across some of the feel, tone and mood you would like to create in your production.

- Involve everyone in the group. It should be clear to the audience that everyone has contributed to the presentation, so everyone should have a part to play.

- Always state your aim to the audience in some way. They will only be able to give a useful evaluation of your work if you have made your aim clear to them.

PRESENTATION METHODS

POWERPOINT PRESENTATION

PowerPoint and other presentation packages are really useful tools for getting your ideas across to an audience. If you choose this method, make sure that you explain your reasoning so far, show character cards and story outlines and use examples and references. You could show images or film clips that have inspired you, or that demonstrate the mood or style you are hoping to achieve. If you choose this method, think about using the online presentation tool Prezi, which provides you with some really interesting visual elements to use.

If you use this website, all your presentations will be in the public domain, which means that they are available for anyone to see and use – free of charge. You can, however, keep your work private for a fee, and they offer discounts to teachers and students.

USE A NARRATOR

Don't be limited by the term **presentation**. Remember that drama is a creative performance subject, and this allows you to be very creative with the way you present. Think about having one person in the group narrating the presentation and others taking part in some kind of performance to illustrate what the narrator is saying. They could perform sample scenes, be a character in role for the audience to interview or maybe present a series of **tableaux** to illustrate the story.

30-SECOND SYNOPSIS

If you have several ideas to present, you could act out a 30-second synopsis of each one. Look at the work of the Reduced Shakespeare Company (who perform Shakespeare's plays in 15 minutes) to see how it's done.

AUDIENCE PARTICPATION

Think about setting up the space as an area that the audience can walk around, look at or experience your ideas. They could meet and speak to potential characters, watch film clips or even become involved in a scene. **Promenade** or **immersive productions** like *The Drowned Man: A Hollywood Fable* and *You Me Bum Bum Train* do this as performances where the audience walks through a building or a location with the drama occurring around them. They have the opportunity to get involved in the drama and shape the performance (or their experience of it) by choosing a story to follow.

ONLINE

Head to www. brightredbooks.net/N5Drama and follow the link to Prezi.

VIDEO LINK

Check out the Reduced Shakespeare Company's version of Hamlet at www. brightredbooks.net/N5Drama

contd

RECEIVING FEEDBACK

There are different ways of requesting feedback from your audience. You can simply ask if there are any questions or comments at the end of your presentation and have a discussion with your audience. This can be very useful, as you can clarify anything that the audience felt was unclear and ask for specific feedback about elements that you are unsure about. If you take this approach you must remember to write down the results of your feedback very soon afterwards, so you have a record of what was discussed.

Alternatively, you could provide your audience with a feedback form to complete. This will allow you to ask specific questions and measure the response. It is also a ready-made record of the feedback that can go into your support log. A combination of the two approaches might be a good way of collecting a good range of responses.

Don't take feedback personally. It can be upsetting to hear that something didn't work out as you had hoped, but try to see it as a way of helping you to improve. If it is constructive criticism, it should help you to understand what worked and why, and what you could do to make your work even better. There is more guidance on giving feedback and constructive criticism in the chapter on reflection and evaluating (pp 38–39).

DON'T FORGET

Technology can enhance a performance or presentation but it doesn't always work perfectly.

DON'T FORGET

Be prepared. Spontaneity is great, but you will do a much better job if you are feeling confident – and preparation is key to this.

ONLINE TEST

Test yourself on presenting ideas at www.brightredbooks.net/N5Drama

THINGS TO DO AND THINK ABOUT

Before your presentation, check that any technology you are using (such as computers and projectors) is working correctly and that your presentation plays on the equipment.

If you are using technology and are relying on film clips or projected images, make sure you have a backup plan if the technology doesn't work.

Be discerning about the criticism you receive. While there might be some great ideas for you to consider, there might also be some things that you don't agree with. Explore everything that's said and take on board the parts that you think will help you. Discard the rest. You don't have to incorporate everything that's offered.

DIRECTING

During your course, you might have an opportunity to direct a performance or a small section of your group's performance. This is a challenging thing to do, but it can be very rewarding. The most important thing with directing is to be prepared and organised. If you are directing a scene, you are responsible for the interpretation and vision of that scene and how it can be realised in the performance. You will need to know the scene or play well, have done your research and have a **concept**. A **directorial concept** is an idea of how the performance elements such as voice, movement and theatre conventions work together with production elements such as lighting design, set, sound and costume to convey a certain message or idea. This will reflect and emphasise the themes and issues of a drama, its characters, **mood**, **atmosphere** and **tension**.

THE DIRECTOR'S ROLE

The director's role in a production includes interpreting the script or scenario, creating design concepts, communicating with the actors and design team, **casting**, **blocking** and organising the rehearsal process. If you are only directing a section of a play, some of these decisions will already have been made for you and you will need to ensure that your section fits with the rest of the production.

If you have responsibility for directing a scene, find out the following and make notes in your support log:

- Who is the audience for this performance?
- What are the possible themes in this scene?
- Which themes and ideas do I want to focus on in this scene and why?
- How can the actors communicate my directorial concepts?
- How can I use other dramatic **techniques** and **conventions** to communicate my ideas?
- What problems might I come up against?

WHAT KIND OF DIRECTOR ARE YOU?

There are a variety of styles of directing. The kind of director you are will probably be decided largely by your experience of being directed, but it is useful to give some thought to your directing style.

THE DICTATOR

In this style of directing, the director takes full control and dictates every step of the process of creating a play. Rehearsals follow a strict pattern and the actors are not consulted about their opinion.

THE COLLABORATOR

The collaborator invites ideas from the cast and production team and the drama is shaped in a democratic way. This style of direction usually involves a lot of improvisation and discussion to explore themes and characters and create a shared vision.

THE CREATIVE

The creative is half-way between the dictator and the collaborator. The creative invites ideas from the creative team, but has a strong vision and reserves the right to have the final say over what is included in the show.

If you are going to take a particular approach, discuss this with your cast and crew beforehand.

DIRECTING TIPS

DEALING WITH DISAGREEMENTS

Disagreements are common when you are working with a group on a creative project. Be prepared to try out the ideas of others – they might just be brilliant. If not, be clear with your vision and why you decide to go another way. If your concept is strong, you will always have a reason and an argument for making a certain decision.

COMMUNICATION

Communication skills are essential to this role. You need to communicate your vision to the actors and crew so they all know what you are aiming towards. Have a clear intention for each rehearsal and communicate this, too. Then, create the right kind of environment for what you are trying to achieve. If you create a positive environment in rehearsals, your team is likely to respond positively. If you want them to contribute ideas, you will need to create an open and friendly atmosphere where people feel safe to do this.

BE REFLECTIVE

You will need to reflect on your experience as a director, so ask for and respond to feedback. You could discuss each rehearsal at the end with your cast, and make notes about what worked well for them and what you could improve. If this turns into an uncomfortable experience, then you could ask them to write their comments down so you can read them later. Remember – this is a shared learning experience and feedback should be constructive and positive. Keep in mind that everyone works in a different way and that you are unlikely to be able to satisfy everyone all of the time.

BE RESPECTFUL

You are there to bring all the elements together, but everyone else has an important job to do too. If you demonstrate that you respect the work they do, it will create a positive atmosphere. Use praise often and suggest trying things another way if it's not quite what you wanted.

MAKE NOTES

During the final rehearsals, try to let the cast do a full run through, rather than interrupting all the time. Remember to take notes. You won't remember everything you want to mention, so have a script with you and write on it where you notice an area for improvement. Have a session after the run through where you give the cast your notes and discuss any changes necessary. The last **director's notes** should be after the **dress rehearsal**.

MAKE IT FUN

There are always times when members of the cast and crew can't be at rehearsals for whatever reason. Be sensitive: people do get ill and sometimes there are other important things they have to do, so have contingency plans. Above all, if you make it really fun and positive they will want to be there.

DON'T FORGET

There will always be problems. Your cast and crew will be able to help: be flexible and creative.

DON'T FORGET

It can be difficult to direct your friends because you are entering into a different – possibly confusing – type of relationship. It might be easier to work with a cast of actors you don't know so well – possibly from a different year group.

THINGS TO DO AND THINK ABOUT

Start small. If you think you might be interested in directing, volunteer or ask to direct a scene or a very short piece of drama first. It is very challenging to go into directing a whole play having never done it before.

See how you get on directing a scene and reflect on it. Record in your support log the parts you thought were really successful and those that didn't work quite as well as you had hoped. Think about alternative approaches you could take on your next attempt. Also include how you sought and responded to feedback from other members of the group.

ONLINE TEST

Test your knowledge of directing at www. brightredbooks.net/N5Drama

DRAMA STRUCTURE

In drama, **structure** is the way in which the story is split into sections, and the way time, place and action are organised within the play.

ACTS AND SCENES

Most plays are split into **acts** and **scenes**. An act is a large division and might be a group of scenes that all relate to the same theme. There are usually two to five acts in a play, although there are some short plays that only have one act. Scenes are smaller divisions and there can be any number of scenes in an act. There is usually a change of scene each time there is a jump in time or place.

TIME

In terms of time structure, all narratives can be split into two broad groups: **linear** or **chronological** and **non-linear**.

LINEAR/CHRONOLOGICAL

This is a naturalistic approach where events happen one after the other in the order they would occur in reality. Time is chronological and the narrative follows a beginning, middle and end structure.

Many plays of this type follow some kind of variation on the classic **dramatic arc** structure. This structure has five stages:

1 **Exposition** – This introduces the main characters and sets the scene. The time and place of the action becomes apparent in this section.

2 **Rising action** – This section introduces some kind of **conflict** that increases the **dramatic tension**. The intensity of the conflict and tension grows until it reaches the climax.

3 **Climax** – This section is where the conflict reaches a point where something changes. It is usually a turning point of some kind. It could be good or bad.

4 **Falling action** – This is the beginning of a resolution where problems begin to be solved and questions are answered.

5 **Resolution** – The final conclusion. It may or may not be a happy ending, but there is some kind of resolution.

Many older classical plays follow this structure and sometimes have five acts, so each act relates to one of the sections of the dramatic arc. Many modern plays have fewer acts and organise the narrative into only two or three acts.

contd

NON-LINEAR

This is a structure in which events do not follow each other in time order. The play might be made up of fragments or it could include **flashbacks** and **flashforwards** that disrupt the normal order of things. The opening scene might be the end of the story and the events that lead up to that final event are slowly revealed.

A non-linear structure might also use pattern or repetition, when one event or phrase is repeated at intervals throughout the drama – as in Samuel Becket's **absurdist** play *Waiting for Godot*. Place and time in absurdist and **surrealist** plays are often ambiguous and dreamlike.

A non-linear play could also be structured into episodes that show actions or events that take place simultaneously, often illustrated by a symbol such as a clock or calendar that shows the date and time of each event. A narrator could also be used to communicate complicated timelines to an audience.

The play *Death of a Salesman* by Arthur Miller is an example of a non-linear narrative.

CONFLICT AND CONTRAST

Your drama will need some kind of **conflict** to make it interesting to the audience. The conflict does not have to be a conflict between characters: it could be a difficult decision that a character has to make or an event that causes problems, like a murder or a hurricane. Conflict in this context really means some kind of problem or issue that needs to be resolved.

Contrast is important when devising drama. Scene after scene of the same type can become boring. Try to vary the pace of scenes. Instead of putting lots of emotional scenes together, or several scenes with lots of dialogue, try alternating between dialogue and action.

ONLINE

Learn more about flashbacks and flashforwards at www.brightredbooks.net/N5Drama

DON'T FORGET

When devising drama, you don't have to use a linear structure. You could include flashbacks to help explain elements of the plot, or use repetition to emphasise a particular event.

DON'T FORGET

Rehearsal is for trying out how things will work for an audience as well as for the actors. Try to consider if a scene works and, if not, cut it out. Don't be afraid to cut something that doesn't add to the drama.

ONLINE TEST

Practise identifying elements of drama structure in the online test at www.brightredbooks.net/N5Drama

THINGS TO DO AND THINK ABOUT

1   Try taking a story you know well such as a children's fairy tale or fable, and alter the structure. Insert some flashbacks and flashforwards, instead of sticking to linear action. Or you could pick an element of the story that you feel is very important and repeat it at intervals throughout the story to emphasise its importance. Or start with the final scene and gradually reveal how events led to that conclusion.

2   Working with a small group of four or five, use an interesting image as inspiration. It could be a photograph or perhaps a painting. Each member of the group has to use the image as inspiration for a scene. It can be literal or abstract. The group then has to devise a narrative to weave all the scenes into one play. It could be that there is only one recurring character linking the scenes, or that each scene is happening to different people, but simultaneously. How will you communicate this to the audience?

THEATRE TECHNIQUES AND CONVENTIONS

Theatre techniques and conventions are elements used in a performance to enhance the storytelling or to aid the understanding of the audience. They can also be used to create a certain style within the production and contribute towards mood and atmosphere. Choosing the correct conventions for your drama is crucial to making your story flow and ensuring that the audience understands what is going on.

ONLINE

There is an example of cross cutting at www.brightredbooks.net/N5Drama

KEY CONVENTIONS

ASIDE

An aside is when a character makes a remark or a short speech to the audience, which is unheard by the other characters on stage. Shakespeare used this extensively in his plays.

CHORAL SPEECH

This is an important element of **Greek drama**. It involves a group of people speaking in unison, acting as the **Chorus**.

CROSS-CUTTING

Cross-cutting is a sequence of scenes that jump backwards and forwards in time and 'cut across' each other.

DRAMATIC IRONY

This is a very effective technique for heightening **tension.** It involves the audience being aware of something that the characters on stage don't know – for example, when Romeo finds Juliet unconscious he thinks she is dead, but the audience knows she is not. This makes it all the more agonising and tragic for the audience when he then kills himself.

FLASHBACK

A flashback is a scene that shows events leading up to the present time. It breaks the chronological sequence of events and moves the action back in time. There must be clues provided for the audience that the timeline has shifted so they understand what is happening. This can be done through **dialogue**, music or movement.

FLASHFORWARD

As with a flashback, a flashforward moves the action through time but this time the action jumps to a point in the future.

FREEZE FRAME

This is a moment in the action when all the actors on stage freeze. It allows the audience to take in more information about what's going on. It can be a useful technique for portraying violent events like a car accident or a fight. You can freeze just a split second after the characters have realised what's about to occur, and leave the audience to imagine the rest.

MIME

Mime could be a short sequence or a whole show performed through physical movement alone without dialogue. This can be useful for setting the context of a scene. It could have musical accompaniment to set the mood and tone, but silence is also powerful and creates **contrast** if you are also using dialogue.

contd

MONOLOGUE

A monologue is a passage of text that a character speaks as if they are speaking their thoughts aloud to other characters or to the audience. This is not to be confused with **soliloquy** below.

MOTIFS

A motif is a recurring element that has symbolic significance in the story. It could be an object, words or sounds but it is repeated many times throughout the performance to tie events together or demonstrate significance.

NARRATION

Narration is when parts of the story are told by a narrator.

SLOW MOTION

Slow motion involves actions being performed at a slowed-down speed. Again, this can be useful for very dramatic or active parts of a performance like fight scenes or chases.

SOLILOQUY

A soliloquy is when a character speaks their thoughts aloud. This differs from a **monologue** in that they are speaking to themselves and not to another character or to the audience.

SYMBOLS

Symbolism in theatre involves using a prop or an element of set or costume to represent an idea. For example, white could symbolise innocence or a flower could symbolise love.

TABLEAU

A tableau is a living picture. The actors create a still image to show an action, idea or moment in a story.

VOICE-OVER

A voice-over can be off stage, or recorded speech played during the production.

THINGS TO DO AND THINK ABOUT

Each member of your group should choose one convention to research. You should find an example of that technique in a play or a film and create a presentation for the rest of the class, explaining why you think the playwright or director chose to use that technique, and the impact it has. This will help you to understand the effect of conventions on mood, atmosphere and audience response.

As a warm-up exercise, experiment with the different techniques by improvising, or by using one or more of them in quickly prepared scenes. For example, you could create a comedy sketch where you have to use slow motion.

Try out all the conventions above, but don't overload your performance by throwing everything in if it's not necessary. Think about different ways of doing things. Do you need a narrator? Could a soliloquy or a monologue do the same job?

If you are using a text where the playwright has included some of these conventions within the play or in the stage directions, consider why they have chosen to do this. Understanding this will help your performance of the piece, because you will be trying to achieve the same effect.

REFLECTING AND EVALUATING

Reflecting and evaluating are important skills in National 5 Drama and they allow you to take responsibility for your own learning. Your support log is an essential tool in the reflection process but you will also take part in many discussions with your group and your teacher that will help you to reflect on and evaluate your progress.

REFLECTION AND EVALUATION: AN OVERVIEW

Reflection means serious thought or consideration. It involves thinking back over an experience and analysing it to learn from it. Without reflection, you are simply having experiences and not really learning anything. Through reflection, you consolidate what you have learned and understand what is required to improve and continue developing your skills.

Evaluation means making a judgement about the value or quality of something. You will be asked in your final examination to evaluate a performance or production that you have been part of, so it is important to develop this skill and practise it throughout your course.

When you evaluate your performance, you will need to consider whether your decisions and performance were effective in achieving your aim or whether there was room for improvement.

By reflecting on and evaluating your work and performance, you continue learning and making improvements to your work and performance: it's a constant and ongoing part of your course.

SELF-EVALUATION

This is not just describing **what** you did – although a brief description is useful. You also need to mention **why** you decided to do that and **what** you hoped to achieve. If your performance was successful, can you identify what made it work and if it wasn't, how could you improve it? You're not only thinking about your own performance, but the development of the production as a whole.

Get into the habit of reflecting on every drama session. Have a section in your log book where you record your thoughts during these reflections.

contd

QUESTIONS TO ASK YOURSELF

What was I trying to achieve?

Did I succeed?

What went well?

What did I find challenging?

Why do I think this was?

What do I think I can do to improve?

Don't be afraid to record the things that don't go so well: you will do better in your course if you can show that you learn from your experiments.

PEER EVALUATION

You will probably be asked to comment on or evaluate the work of your fellow students many times during your course. Remember to keep your feedback sensitive, positive and constructive and focus on the work.

THINGS TO DO AND THINK ABOUT

As a group, role-play really bad ways to give other people feedback. If you keep it lighthearted, this will help everyone to understand how **not** to do it, and it will reinforce the importance of being sensitive and positive with your comments.

Think about giving feedback to others in the form of written comments, possibly as an annotated script – like a director's notes. This will give the performer the opportunity to reflect on the feedback in private. Again, always phrase it positively. Praise the good and suggest ideas to try.

As a class, you could set up a suggestion box in the studio. When performing work in progress to an audience, verbal feedback could be restricted to positive comments, so the audience must identify only what worked well in the performance. They can then write down and post in the box any suggestions they have for improvements at any time. This could be emptied weekly, with suggestions passed on to the groups concerned.

VIDEO LINK

The video at www.brightredbooks.net/N5Drama explains how you can self-evaluate.

DON'T FORGET

Self-evaluation and reflection feels strange at first if you are not used to it. It does take practice before you feel comfortable with it and you start to see results. Don't give up.

DON'T FORGET

When giving someone else feedback, think about how you would feel if someone said it to you. If you would be upset, then think of another, more positive, way to put it.

ONLINE

There is a good example of self-evaluation online at www.brightredbooks.net/N5Drama

ONLINE TEST

How well have you learned about reflecting and evaluating? Test yourself at www.brightredbooks.net/N5Drama

DRAMA SKILLS

PROBLEM-SOLVING

While developing your drama work you will inevitably encounter problems! This is not a bad thing; in fact it is very good. One of the major assessment criteria for National 5 Drama is to show how you approach and overcome problems. The key to problem-solving is a positive attitude and a creative approach. In a sense, drama is one long series of problems to be solved – for example:

How do you make the audience believe the characters?

How do you tell the story in an engaging way?

How do you make a character fly, or appear as a ghost?

HOW TO DO IT

CHANGE YOUR THINKING

Try to see a problem as an interesting challenge rather than a difficulty. It's an opportunity to use your skills and be creative. There are always solutions – you just have to try them out. Problems become much easier to solve if you approach them in this way. And don't be afraid to fail! Failure is also a positive thing. If a possible solution doesn't work, think about why, learn from it, and move on to the next idea.

PRACTICE

You can practise problem-solving behaviour with your group by playing games. This is a fun way to develop supportive, creative relationships where you listen to each other and share ideas, try things out, fail and learn.

Here are some games you might like to try.

 ACTIVITY: ELECTRIC FENCE

Two groups play against each other. You need a space a little wider than one team standing side-by-side. One team has to form an electric fence with their bodies spanning the space. They must do this in 60 seconds without speaking. The other team faces away from the fence until it is constructed. They then have three minutes to get all team members across, over, through or under the fence without touching it. They must also do this without speaking to each other. If any member of the team touches the fence, they are electrocuted and the team has failed. Swap roles.

ACTIVITY: BLINDFOLD LINE-UP

Each group member wears a blindfold. Without speaking to each other, you have to line up in order of birthday. You could also do this in order of height, by shoe size or alphabetically.

ACTIVITY: CROSSED/UNCROSSED

This game works well when only one or two people know the rule, because the aim of the game is for everyone to figure out the rule. The rule can be anything, really, but it will often relate to legs.

So, for example, everyone sits in a circle and one person starts off by passing a pair of scissors to the person on their left. If the person passing the scissors has crossed their legs, or the person to whom they are passing the scissors has crossed their legs, they would say: 'I am passing these scissors to you crossed' (or 'I am passing these scissors to you uncrossed' if their legs aren't crossed). The next person does the same and the first person will confirm if they are correct or not. The scissors can be open or closed and you can deliberately change the way you pass them to throw people off the scent.

contd

 **ACTIVITY:** SUPERHEROES

This is an improvisation game, where suggestions are taken from the group.

One person enters the performance space. They are given a problem by the audience, preferably something silly such as 'your shoelaces are untied' or 'you have put your cardigan on back to front' – but they can't solve it by themselves. The audience then suggests an object like 'toothpaste' or 'lamp'.

Another player then enters the improvisation as a superhero related to that object, so 'lamp man' comes to save the day and helps to solve the problem. The two players must work together to figure out how to solve the problem using the superhero's special power.

Whenever you have a difficult problem to solve, play a game like this first to get to get into the right frame of mind.

EXPERIMENT

Sometimes you make so many changes along the way that your story doesn't make sense or has some holes in it. If this happens, try telling the story backwards, experiment with techniques like **flashbacks** and **flashforwards** to help it along, add in a **narrator** to explain what's happening or have a character speak their thoughts in an **aside**. If you feel you need an extra scene, improvise some ideas first and see what happens. You will find the answer if you experiment and play with it.

Have a look at the section about working with others (pp 6–7) for more advice on how to tackle problems.

 THINGS TO DO AND THINK ABOUT

There will always be unexpected problems when staging a production but you can minimise them by thinking ahead and having back-up plans. During your rehearsal stage, make a list of risks. Try to think of all the things that could go wrong and figure out how you will cope if they happen. This will help you to think through problems before they occur.

In rehearsal, make sure you occasionally run scenes through without stopping, even if someone forgets a line, misses an entrance or makes a mistake. Try not to break character and to react in role. This is an important performance skill and it's really useful to develop strategies to manage these situations.

 ONLINE

For more great ideas for problem-solving games, head to www.brightredbooks.net/N5Drama

 DON'T FORGET

Be flexible. It is fine to completely change your plan if an interesting solution presents itself.

 DON'T FORGET

Document all the problems you encounter and how you solved them in your support log.

 ONLINE TEST

Take the 'Problem-solving' test at www.brightredbooks.net/N5Drama

CHARACTERISATION

If you are acting in a drama piece, you will be portraying a character who is different from you. To be convincing, you will need to develop the character and get to know them well. This process is called **characterisation**.

Get to know your character and find out what their **motivation** is. Think about their history, hobbies, likes and dislikes or family situation – these are elements of everyone's life and it will help you to make your character convincing for the audience.

VOICE AND MOVEMENT

The **dialogue** is not the only way that character is communicated to an audience. Voice and body language also communicate a great deal so it is important to consider these when developing your character. For example, think about how you can tell straightaway, even before they have spoken a word, that someone is very shy. They might keep their head down or stand in a way that suggests they are very self-conscious.

The same applies to voice. Even if someone is saying that they are fine you can quite often tell that they are really upset by their tone of voice.

 **ACTIVITY**

Consider your character's voice. How might it differ from your own? Would they use vocabulary you would perhaps not use? For example, they might speak very formally or use more slang. Also consider their body language. Would they stand up straighter, do they have a limp, a nervous tick, or are they aggressive? What are the reasons for this?

SUSTAINING THE ROLE

Once you have developed your character, it is important for the performance that you **sustain the role**. This means that while you are performing you stay in character and don't **corpse**. **Corpsing** is breaking character and becoming yourself during the performance. This can be caused by things such as forgetting lines, giggling at something or becoming stuck with an improvisation. If you know your character well, it will be easier to sustain the role because you will be able to cope with unexpected events in role and improvise to overcome them.

Useful characterisation techniques to develop character include:

- **Hot-seating** – being interviewed in role about background, likes and dislikes, thoughts and emotions.
- **Role-play** – improvising in role in different scenarios to explore how the character would act in different situations.
- Ask a friend to read your lines aloud while you concentrate on movement and **body language**. This will help you to focus on communicating your character's thoughts through facial expression and action alone.
- Try using a **prop** or a piece of **costume** to get into character. Whenever you hold the prop or wear the costume, you are in role.
- **Thought tunnel** – This can be used in a variety of ways. The group forms two lines facing each other and one person (in role) walks slowly through the tunnel while the people on either side speak their thoughts aloud. The thoughts could be what they imagine the character is thinking or what other characters in the drama think of the character in the middle.
- **Writing in role** – write a diary entry or a letter as if you are the character. This will help you to explore the thoughts that the character has about other characters, or the action of the drama.
- **Thought tracking** – freeze the action during rehearsal and speak the thoughts of a character aloud.

THINGS TO DO AND THINK ABOUT

1. **Create a character card:** Create headings that give personal information about your character. Include name, age, occupation, family, hobbies, likes and dislikes. You can add to this as your character develops and you learn more about them.

2. **Experiment with body language:** Play the adverb game. One member of the group leaves the room while the rest decide upon an adverb – for example lazily, snootily, confidently or shyly. The absent member of the group is called back in and asks the group to mime an action. It could be something simple such as brushing teeth or eating, or something more involved like fixing a bike. The rest of the group must perform the action silently using only facial expression and body language to convey the adverb. The other member of the group must try to guess from the actions what the adverb is. Use this activity to think about the adverb that best describes your character, and practice conveying this adverb through facial expression and body language.

3. **Experiment with voice:** Introduce your character using different voices. For example, speak very formally, very fast, much slower than normal, hesitantly (with lots of 'ums' and 'urs') very loud and confidently or very quietly and shyly. Which voice suits your character best?

4. **Write in role:** Imagine you are your character and write a letter to another character in the drama. Include how your character really feels about an incident that occurs in the drama or how they feel about other characters.

At this end of this process you should be getting a feel for your character. Develop your character further with the techniques listed above.

VIDEO LINK

See thought tracking in action at www. brightredbooks.net/N5Drama

DON'T FORGET

Movement and body language communicates as much as your speech. Think carefully about how your character would stand and move.

DON'T FORGET

It can sometimes be necessary or useful for the drama to play an unpleasant character - but they should still be convincing. Give some thought to the character's **motivations** and history. Why is the character so unpleasant?

ONLINE TEST

Check what you know about developing a character with the quiz at www. brightredbooks.net/N5Drama

MOOD AND ATMOSPHERE

CREATING TENSION

Creating the appropriate mood and atmosphere is crucial to the success of a performance. The more an audience is transported by your story, the more successful it is. Creating an emotional response in the audience means that they are absorbed in your drama and they care what happens to the characters, so that, for example, when you build up **tension,** they become hopeful, scared or excited. This keeps the audience interested in what is happening on stage and gives the drama momentum.

You can create mood and atmosphere in a theatrical production through the:

- content of the drama
- acting techniques
- production techniques.

You can find ideas for production techniques on (pp 66–79).

In this section, we'll look at how you can create tension through the content of your drama or the way you perform it.

CONTENT

Try using these elements as part of your storytelling to affect the mood and atmosphere and build the **dramatic tension.**

- **Action** – The events that characters take part in during the story. It is important to include action as well as dialogue for **contrast**.

- **Conflict and confrontation** –This could be external or internal conflict that rises to a confrontation of some kind. Have a look at the chapter on selecting ideas (pp 28–29) for more information about conflict.

- **Dramatic irony** – This is when the audience knows something that the characters on stage do not: for example, the audience knows that Viola in Shakespeare's *Twelfth Night* is a woman disguised as a man.

- **Mystery** – This involves creating an atmosphere of suspense by presenting the audience with questions and clues.

- **Relationships and status** – The relationships between people – for example, a 'will-they-won't-they' love story or a power struggle – can create different atmospheres and types of tension.

- **Surprise** – This could be a twist in the tale, something completely unexpected or perhaps a shocking revelation.

- **Silence** – If you are writing a script or creating a story, don't forget the silences. Silent moments or sequences are important to set mood and tone and, if done well, can draw the audience in.

- **Threat or pressure** – A sense of danger in some form can add to the tension and atmosphere of a story. For example, it could be physical danger or the threat of losing a business, money or loved one.

ACTING

These performance techniques are ways that you can change and affect the atmosphere while on stage. They are very powerful, and you should consider each one in rehearsal to enhance your performance.

contd

- **Contrast** – This could be between activity and stillness, action and dialogue, quiet and loud. If every scene contained the same elements at the same level, it would be difficult to maintain the audience's interest.

- **Eye contact** – The way you use eye contact helps to portray relationships on stage and can increase the dramatic tension. Focused eye contact can be quite tense or very intimate. Avoiding eye contact can be uncomfortable and seem suspicious.

- **Intent/focus** – This refers to how you focus the audience's attention **and** to your own focus as a performer. You are in control of how you focus the audience's attention through your own skill as a performer. Your focus as a performer is an important factor in creating a believable character. If you believe in your character and you are confident in your performance, the audience will suspend its disbelief. If you are unfocused and seem unsure, your performance will not be convincing.

- **Movement** – The way the actors move around the performance area can have a huge effect on mood and atmosphere. Fast, furious movement can create a sense of urgency or danger, while more fluid, natural movement can make the audience feel relaxed and comfortable. Think about the way you move to create **contrast**.

- **Pace** – This is the momentum, or rhythm, of the performance. If you want the audience to be surprised and uncomfortable, use jarring sequences to break the momentum of the rhythm.

- **Pause** – These moments of silence are very effective for setting mood. You can use pauses to create a tense atmosphere, so the audience is almost holding its breath, waiting for something to happen.

- **Physical contact** – Like eye contact, this can be an effective way to express status and relationships. Depending on how you do this, it can be uncomfortable, threatening or affectionate.

- **Positioning** – This could be the positioning of the audience or the performers. Where you position the audience in relation to the performance will have an effect on the atmosphere. Do you want them to feel involved in the action or removed from it? The positioning of actors on stage, or in the audience, also allows you to affect atmosphere.

- **Silence and stillness** – These are important elements to consider as both are essential for creating contrast. Don't feel that a performance has to be constant motion and sound. You can create intensity and surprises with clever use of silence and stillness.

- **Timing** – This applies to both dialogue and action. You can create a tense atmosphere or a frantic, chaotic one by changing the timing of action and dialogue. Getting the timing right is also crucial for comedy to work.

- **Voice** – This is not only about storytelling and expressing emotion, but also about using techniques to manipulate the audience experience – for example, using a softer (but still audible) volume for tense moments to make the audience listen more closely, or creating a silence before the storm, or everyone shouting at once to create an atmosphere of chaos and turmoil.

ONLINE

Revise mood and atmosphere at www.brightredbooks.net/N5Drama

DON'T FORGET

Production elements also contribute to creating the mood and atmosphere of a production. Think about how costumes, lights, make-up and sound can contribute to mood and atmosphere.

 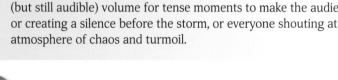

THINGS TO DO AND THINK ABOUT

As you are rehearsing a scene, consider each one of the acting techniques above for your character. For example, where would your character be in relation to the other characters? What level of eye contact would they make with each other? Make a note of the decisions you make in your support log along with the reasons why.

ONLINE TEST

Check what you know about mood and atmosphere with the test at www.brightredbooks.net/N5Drama

VOICE

As a performer, your voice is an important tool and, along with your body, your main method of communicating with the audience. Think of your voice as an instrument that you must look after and practise to be able to use effectively. Professional actors take great care of their voices, because without them, their job would be impossible. It is like an important muscle for an athlete. If you will be using your voice a great deal in a performance, it is important to warm-up properly beforehand and to rest when necessary. If you are rehearsing just before a performance, use only fifty percent of your vocal capability to save your voice for the performance. This is particularly important if you are also singing.

WARM-UP IDEAS

CHEWY TOFFEE

To warm-up the muscles of the face and mouth, imagine you have a really chewy toffee. Unwrap it and put it in your mouth and begin to chew. It will get stuck all round your teeth. Exaggerate the chewing motion as much as you can. This works best done as a group standing in a circle so you can see everyone.

ZOOM

Zoom is a useful game for warming up the voice, practising projecting your voice and speaking from your diaphragm. Sit or stand in a circle. One person starts passing the sound around by saying 'zoom' and turning their head in the direction they want the sound to go. Others continue the sound in the same direction until someone says 'eek' which puts on the brakes and sends the zoom back in the other direction. You can also say 'bang' and point across the circle to someone else, who then chooses the direction for the 'zoom'. It should be fast and loud!

SOUNDSCAPES

Creating a soundscape is a good way to experiment and play with mood and atmosphere, as well as to warm-up voices. First, choose a location or setting – for example, a circus or a beach, or somewhere with distinctive sounds. Stand in a circle with your eyes closed. One person starts by making a sound related to that place and each person joins in, in turn, around the circle until the sound builds and layers to create a soundscape of that place.

ELEMENTS OF VOICE

When you are thinking about the voice of a character, there are several things you need to consider about what they say and how they say it.

LANGUAGE

If you are using a text, the words are given to you, but if you are devising your drama think about the type of language your character would use. Word choice and order are as important as the sound of your voice. Would their language be formal or informal? Would they try to use complicated words that they don't really understand? Would they swear a lot? If you are playing a historical character, think about using language appropriate to the period and their status.

PROJECTING VOICE

As a performer, it can be useful to learn how to control your breathing and use your diaphragm for speaking as this helps to project your voice if you are performing in a large space where your voice may get lost. Practise breathing deeply into your belly and

contd

VIDEO LINK

There is a useful video from the BBC about the importance of warming up your voice and one from the National Theatre about the importance of breathing at www.brightredbooks.net/N5Drama

VIDEO LINK

Check out the clip at www.brightredbooks.net/N5Drama for great advice on projecting your voice.

pushing the air up from there. If you put your hands on your stomach just below your rib cage, you should be able to feel this happening. This takes practice and will probably feel strange at first, but it is a very useful performance skill.

COMMUNICATING CHARACTER AND EMOTION

Everyone uses their voice in different ways. Start listening to how they do this, and how their voices change. For example, many people have a 'telephone voice' that tends to be more formal and polite than their normal speaking voice. People's voices often become tighter or 'wobble' when they are upset and trying to control themselves. Think also about variations of speech, such as stutters and lisps and whether these would be useful for your character.

KEY WORDS

Accent – a particular way of pronouncing words that is related to a place or area.

Articulation – forming clear and distinct sounds – not running words together.

Clarity – words are clear and can be understood.

Dialogue – a conversation between two or more people as part of a book, play or film.

Emphasis – stress given to a word or phrase to demonstrate importance.

Fluency – speech flowing effortlessly and smoothly.

Intonation – the rise and fall of the voice when speaking.

Pace – the speed of the speech.

Pause – a temporary break in speech or dialogue – a short period of silence.

Pitch – how high or low the voice is.

Projection – the ability to make your voice heard at a distance.

Register – appropriate speech and language for the situation and purpose.

Timing – speaking at the appropriate moment for the purpose.

Tone – the type of feeling or mood being expressed.

Volume – the loudness or softness of the voice.

THINGS TO DO AND THINK ABOUT

Rehearse your own scene with a partner using only the word 'sausage'. Decide on a situation and what might happen and keep it fairly simple. Rehearse just as you would normally, and keep the emphasis, tone and intonation of normal speech, but replace all dialogue with the word 'sausage'. When you perform this in front of an audience, you have done a good job if they can understand either the emotions involved, or what is happening.

Cut out a selection of images of different characters from magazines. Each group member could choose one at random and compose a short monologue for them. You should consider the appropriate language to use and then consider each of the vocal elements above to suit the character. Perform the monologues for each other and discuss your impressions and the challenges. Remember that there is really no right and wrong and that two people might give a very different voice to the same character.

ONLINE

There is some useful advice about voice online at www.brightredbooks.net/N5Drama

VIDEO LINK

There are a number of useful videos about voice at www.brightredbooks.net/N5Drama

DON'T FORGET

The way you stand and move will have an effect on your voice. Be careful not to restrict or muffle your sound accidentally.

DON'T FORGET

Accents are very difficult. Only use one if you are confident you can maintain it convincingly (unless you are trying to be funny!)

ONLINE TEST

Test yourself on voice skills at www.brightredbooks.net/N5Drama

MOVEMENT

Movement in drama is a way of exploring and expressing ideas, emotions and relationships. Like your voice, your body is an important tool in communicating with the audience, and there are a variety of skills and techniques you can develop and practise to help with this.

There are two types of movement in drama: **naturalistic** and **stylised**. Naturalistic movement is the way you would move in normal life. In drama, this is used as an aid to characterisation, to demonstrate status and show emotion and relationships. Stylised movement is more about expressing abstract ideas as in dance-drama, mime, physical theatre and mask work.

Whether movement is improvised or rehearsed, it is a key element of your performance.

WARM-UP

Just like your voice, your body needs to be warmed up before you use it, particularly if you are rehearsing a very physical piece. Warming up also helps you to feel connected to every part of your body, which makes it much easier to use it to express character and emotion.

Begin with your head and move down through your body, stretching, flexing and moving each part in turn until you reach your feet. This is a good way to start any session focusing on physical theatre.

NATURALISTIC MOVEMENT

Naturalistic movement is the type of movement a character would make in everyday life and in response to the situations they find themselves in. Everyone moves in a different way and elements of movement such as body language and **gesture** can speak volumes about emotion and status in a scene. Think about the following types of movement when you are developing your character and in rehearsals.

BODY LANGUAGE

If you watch people move, you will see the variety of ways the body communicates without speech.

Think in particular about the difference between **open** and **closed** body language. With open body language, the body is literally open – the arms are not covering the body in a self-protective way, and the palms are often exposed. The character will therefore appear relaxed and confident.

Closed body language on the other hand might involve the character crossing their arms, rounding their shoulders or possibly holding their head down in a self-protective way. The character will therefore appear nervous, shy or scared.

As you are developing your character, make notes in your support log about your choices for body language and the reasons why.

FACIAL EXPRESSION

Your **facial expression** is vital to communicating with the audience, because people will always focus on your face first if they can see it. You obviously can't see your own face, so practise expressions in a mirror and get to know what they feel like. This will help you to control the muscles of your face.

GESTURE

Gesture is an important element of body language, and refers mainly to the hands, but sometimes to other body parts such as the head or feet. Angles of the head such as nodding, shaking, a nod in certain direction or a raise of the chin to indicate a question are also frequently used in non-verbal communication.

VIDEO LINK

Head to www.brightredbooks.net/N5Drama for a helpful video about developing body language for characters.

contd

BE SPECIFIC

Use references that your audience will understand to help them visualise the scene. Because improvisation usually takes place with no set or props, you have to use language and mime to paint the picture for the audience. Use local examples of places where you can give more detail, so instead of saying 'I'll meet you in the cafe' perhaps say 'I'll meet you in 'Joe's Ice Cream Parlour' so the audience have more of an idea of what the setting looks like.

DON'T RUSH

Don't feel that improvisation has to be non-stop dialogue and action. Quite often, improvisation can become frantic and difficult to follow with everyone rushing to get their ideas in. You can include pauses. Sometimes the situation might be quite tense and include long silences where the characters are struggling to communicate with each other.

KEEP IT INTERESTING

When playing improvisation games, change the situation regularly. If nothing has happened for a while say: 'I just realised that...' and add an idea that changes the situation. It can also be an idea to start in the middle of a scene so, rather than introducing yourself to a character and asking who they are when you enter, start with 'Thank God I found you!' and give them something to react to.

ENTRANCES AND EXITS

Entrances and exits should always have a purpose. Enter the scene with an activity or emotion so you have a starting point and a reason for arriving. You might be just a passerby on the street, but you should still have somewhere you are heading and a reason for stopping. If you are leaving the improvisation, you must give a reason – don't just wander off.

OFFER INFORMATION

If an improvisation is getting stuck, offer some new information to get it moving again. Perhaps tell the other person something about their character that they hadn't considered, or say something that they will have to try to explain. For example, say 'nice dress by the way' to a boy or 'what's with the party hat?'

DON'T ASK TOO MANY QUESTIONS

Avoid asking too many questions, because then you are getting the other person to do all the work. Make statements that add information instead. Instead of asking 'who are you?' or 'what are you doing?' decide who they are or what they are doing, and give them the information to respond to – for example, 'I've never seen anyone stuff a cat before!'

STAY IN THE MOMENT

Try to be present in the moment when you are improvising. If you are thinking about what you are having for dinner or your maths exam, you won't perform as well as you could. Relax and focus on what you are doing and the other people involved.

MIME

Quite often you will not have scenery and props when improvising, so mime skills help the audience to visualise what you are doing. Practise your mime skills – this will make your improvisations better. See the chapter on movement for more advice about mime (pp 48–49).

DON'T TRY TO BE FUNNY

Improvisation is often funny but this usually comes from the relationships and unusual situations. Don't try too hard to be funny because if you are concentrating on making the audience laugh you are not focused on the other actors and supporting them.

THINGS TO DO AND THINK ABOUT

There are hundreds of improvisation games and variations on them. Here's a couple to start off with.

Three rules: This is a short improvisation with a group of two or three people, where three rules are assigned for the performance. For example, characters can only have one arm, they have to say 'I can't hear you' after every question that's asked and they cannot use any words that begin with an f. These limitations must be followed, and as soon as someone forgets or breaks one, they are out and replaced by someone else.

Object narrative: This is a great activity for developing character and teamwork. Have a chair in a performance space that is easily visible to everyone. One person chooses an object – anything at all – and then places it on the chair. Whenever someone has an idea, they can go and sit on the chair and perform a short monologue about the object, telling the audience a story that involves it in some way. As soon as they have finished, someone else takes their place and continues the story as a different, but associated character. Be creative with the characters: you don't have to be the previous character's husband or wife – you might be someone they pushed in front of at the bus stop, or their hairdresser.

DON'T FORGET

If you are a supportive and responsive improvisation partner, people will want to work with you and the results will be better.

ONLINE

Have a look at www.brightredbooks.net/N5Drama for more ideas.

ONLINE TEST

Take the "Improvisation Test" at www.brightredbooks.net/N5Drama

PERFORMANCE

The culmination of all your work on the National 5 Drama course will be a **performance**. Throughout the course, you will probably take part in several different performances in various roles, including offstage and backstage roles. This will give you a chance to develop and practise your performance skills.

WORK AS A TEAM

Depending on the nature and size of your production, there could be a variety of people backstage that you will be working with. A performance is a team effort and everyone is vital to its success.

PERFORMANCE TIPS

WARM-UP FIRST

Start warming up about half an hour before you go on stage. This will help to relax you and get your voice and body prepared for what you have to do. It's also useful to have a warm-up to control your nerves. You can do this individually or as a group. Get into character at this point, so you are already thinking and moving like your character when you go on stage.

FOCUS

Once you are in character, try to maintain your focus on what is happening in the present moment. Don't let yourself be distracted by thoughts of what will happen after the show or tomorrow. Whatever happens, try not to **corpse**. Even if you forget a line, improvise in character.

ENERGY

Try to maintain your energy level. Acting on stage takes a great deal of energy, particularly because all of your actions and emotions have to be slightly larger than in real life. The audience responds to the energy you give and it's easy to run out of steam towards the end of the show. Do some stretches backstage if you feel yourself flagging. If you get nervous, you can use and channel that nervous energy into your performance.

DEALING WITH NERVES

There are many ways to deal with nerves and different things work for different people. The most important thing is to make sure that you are prepared. Feeling confident will really help with nerves.

Learn what relaxes you: some people like to listen to music on headphones before a performance and some like to exercise.

You could distract yourself by getting absorbed in something else or spend time alone getting into character.

Nerves are not a negative thing – they are your body's way of preparing you for a challenge and helping you to focus. Just learn how to control them, and don't let them get the better of you.

COMMIT TO THE ROLE

If you believe it, the audience will. You must commit to your role and give it everything you've got. If you look unsure and embarrassed, the audience will be embarrassed for you.

VIDEO LINK

There is a useful video about committing to a role at www.brightredbooks.net/N5Drama

TROUBLESHOOTING

What to do if you are onstage and ...

SOMEONE FORGETS THEIR LINES

Improvise! It happens to everyone at some point. If you have forgotten your lines, you need to stay calm and be present in the moment. Think about what your character's motivation is at that point in time and improvise along those lines. If you know what the point of the scene is, you will be able to get by. If someone else has forgotten their line, give them a minute but don't just stand and look at them. Do something in character in the meantime – perhaps tidy up a bit or look for something. If they don't recover, you can prompt them by asking a question that gives them a clue to the direction of the scene. If they start improvising, respond to it rather than sticking rigidly to the script.

THE PROP YOU NEED IS NOT THERE

Improvise! It will depend on the situation and the context of your scene. You might (in character) be able to ask one of the other characters to go and get it for you if it makes sense to do that. You might also be able to get by without it and just skip that part of the scene if it's incidental. If all else fails, mime that you have it.

THE LIGHTS AREN'T WORKING OR THE SOUND EFFECT IS MISSING

Carry on regardless! Chances are that people are furiously trying to fix something backstage. You just need to carry on with your job until they can sort it out. There's a good chance that the audience won't even notice.

SOMEONE MISSES A CUE

Carry on regardless and improvise! If someone doesn't arrive on stage when they are supposed to, you will need to continue with whatever happens before their arrival. If the situation allows, you might be able to call them but otherwise you have to act as if they were not supposed to enter at that point. If you are doing something, then continue doing it or repeat the last line in different words. Chances are they will arrive and all you have to do is fill time convincingly until that happens.

The show must go on!

THINGS TO DO AND THINK ABOUT

Look after yourself. Preparing for a performance can be very exciting but also quite stressful and everyone's body reacts differently to stress. During rehearsals and as the performance gets closer, make sure you look after yourself properly. Get plenty of sleep, exercise regularly and eat healthily. Drink plenty of water during rehearsals – dehydration can make you tired and unfocused.

Have fun. Whatever the role you are playing in the performance – whether you are acting on stage or as part of the technical team – enjoy the experience. It's a great feeling to work together to create something for an audience. It will be the culmination of a lot of hard work from everyone.

Review your performance. Wait until the next day when you have had a chance to reflect upon your performance and try to identify the parts that worked really well and why, the areas you feel you could have improved and any things that you think you might need to work on a little more.

Leave enough time in your rehearsal schedule for several full 'run-throughs', as well as a dress rehearsal and a technical rehearsal. This will help everyone to cope with the unexpected. Every performance is different, and there will be new problems each time you do it.

DON'T FORGET

Don't rehearse too close to performance. Try to be ready so you can have a rest before the performance and come to it fresh.

DON'T FORGET

Be prepared for the unexpected whatever your role. You might have to be creative and improvise if something goes wrong.

ONLINE TEST

Test how prepared you are for your performance at www.brightredbooks.net/N5Drama

PRODUCTION SKILLS

SECTION OVERVIEW

During the National 5 Drama course you will have the opportunity to learn and develop a variety of production skills. You should try to take on a range of production roles to develop these skills. The chapters on each production role will give you more information about the responsibilities and keywords for each member of the production team.

PRODUCTION ROLES

The production roles you choose will depend to some extent on the equipment available to you at your school or college. You will usually be able to choose two roles from the following list:

- Acting
- Lighting design
- Costume design
- Make-up and hair design
- Properties manager
- Set design
- Sound design

RESPONSIBILITIES

ACTING

Acting is perhaps the role you will know most about and have the most experience of at this point, but it is useful to think about the specific responsibilities of an actor in a production. Your responsibilities are to:

- read the script or extract carefully and make notes on all the characters
- discuss the interpretation of the character with the director and do background research
- attend all the rehearsals
- take direction from the director
- experiment with character, voice and movement to portray character
- learn your lines and blocking
- meet with members of the production team as needed
- play the part and sustain the role in performance.

COSTUME DESIGNER

As the costume designer, you will have to source, adapt or create costumes for the performance. Your responsibilities are to:

- read the script and discuss costume ideas and requirements for all characters with the director
- research the setting, time and the place of the drama
- attend production meetings to liaise with the production team
- make, select or borrow costumes for all characters
- rack and label all costumes
- be available during performances to perform maintenance and help with changes
- check that all costumes are present and in good repair before and after the performance
- return all costumes to the correct place after the performance.

LIGHTING DESIGNER

If your school has a **lighting rig** of more than eight **lanterns**, you may be able to take on the role of lighting designer. As the lighting designer, it is your job to help to create the right mood and atmosphere for the performance. Your responsibilities are to:

- read the script to develop an understanding of the extract or play
- design the lighting for the performance
- attend production meetings and liaise with the design team to ensure the lighting design works with other aspects of design
- create a **lighting plot** and **cue sheet**, **rigging** and **focusing** lighting according to your design
- adjust lighting at the technical rehearsal
- flash through the lights before each performance to check the lamps and focus
- operate lighting during the shows
- **strike** the lighting rig after the performance
- demonstrate an understanding of health and safety when operating lighting equipment.

contd

MAKE-UP AND HAIR DESIGN

As the make-up and hair designer, you will help to communicate character to the audience. The responsibilities of this role are to:

- read the script and discuss each character with the director and the costume designer
- record any allergies that cast members might have to make-up
- design the make-up and hair for all the characters that require it
- complete a **make-up chart** for any characters that need make-up
- create any special make-up effects required
- apply make-up and hair for dress-rehearsals and the performance, and ensure that it is effective.

PROPERTIES MANAGER

The properties manager is responsible for all the props used in the performance. The responsibilities of this role are to:

- read the script and make a **props list**
- attend production meetings and liaise with the production team to make sure that the props list is complete and that all props are appropriate
- source props and note what is taken from where
- provide rehearsal props when required
- create and keep a **props table**
- check before, after and during performances that all props are where they should be
- repair damaged props
- return borrowed props and store others carefully.

SET DESIGNER

As the set designer you will be in charge of how the stage or performance area looks for the performance. Your responsibilities are to:

- read the script
- discuss the interpretation of the text with the director
- design a set in keeping with the **design concept**
- create a **ground plan** and an **elevation** of the set
- consider the size and nature of the performance space and any restrictions
- take health and safety issues into consideration and ensure that the set can be moved as needed
- attend production meetings, oversee the building of the set and **strike** the set at the end of the performance.

SOUND DESIGNER

As the sound designer for the performance, you will add to the mood and atmosphere of the show. Your responsibilities are to:

- read the script and note requirements and ideas for sounds effects and music
- discuss sound effects ideas with the director
- research the period and location to ensure the sounds create the right setting
- have knowledge of the sound equipment and how it is used
- attend production meetings to liaise with all design staff
- organise sound and music during rehearsals to help the actors know their cues
- complete a **sound cue sheet**, source effects, voice-overs and music as necessary and operate the sound during **technical rehearsals** and the performance.

ONLINE

There is a very useful website including videos on many of the different production roles here. You can access this via www.brightredbooks.net/N5Drama

DON'T FORGET

You must use relevant vocabulary in your writing about your drama. Look at the sections about each production role for keywords and vocabulary.

DON'T FORGET

You need to have an overview of all the production roles so make sure you know the responsibilities of each role.

THINGS TO DO AND THINK ABOUT

Try out as many of the production roles as you can during this unit. This will help you to decide what role to take for your final performance. Even if you really enjoy acting, you might discover a hidden talent or passion for costume design or lighting too!

ONLINE TEST

Test yourself on production roles at www.brightredbooks.net/N5Drama

MOOD AND ATMOSPHERE

Production techniques, sometimes called **theatre arts**, play a major part in creating mood and atmosphere in theatre. When staging a play, you are aiming to manipulate the audience reaction, whether you want them to be absorbed and transported by the story or to remain aware of the experience and think about the issues and themes of the play. Careful thought about every element of the performance will help you to encourage your audience to **suspend their disbelief** and become absorbed in the show. Let's take a look at some of the things you should consider when you are creating the mood for your production.

COSTUME DESIGN

An audience receives a great deal of information from costume, as it is an instant visual clue to character, status and time period. Costume design can create a very powerful and striking effect. Naturalistic costumes are very easy for audiences to understand as we make assumptions about people based on what they are wearing all the time. For example, a group of 'hoodies' with hoods pulled up could be quite a threatening presence, or a group of older men in suits would give the impression of power. More stylised costumes can have an unsettling effect as the normal clues are taken away. Techniques such as using all one colour in costume means the audience has to focus much more on the dialogue and acting.

LIGHTING DESIGN

The lighting of a scene can change the mood and atmosphere completely. The same setting can be made warm and comfortable or cold and unwelcoming just by changing the lighting. Colour plays an enormous part in this.

In their simplest forms, colours can represent certain moods and emotions. Mixed, they achieve more subtle effects.

- Red can represent anger, tension, envy, fear or danger.
- Green could be jealousy, but also death and decay.
- Blue is cold and can represent sadness or power.
- Pink is quite a warm and gentle colour. It can represent romance, but shocking pink can be cartoon-like.
- Yellow suggests warmth, calm and sunshine.

You can also use effects such as strobes for unsettling effects or slow motion action.

SOUND DESIGN

MUSIC

Good use of mood music to set a particular tone can enhance or heighten tension in a dramatic performance. If you are using **incidental** music before the show starts, think about whether you want to set the tone straight away or create a jarring comparison.

Think about the different effect of music with lyrics and instrumental music. Will the lyrics in a piece of music fit the theme or story? Give the audience clues as to what's happening or about to happen with the music, or lead them in the wrong direction to surprise them.

SOUND EFFECTS

Clever use of sound effects can heighten tension and encourage the audience to suspend their disbelief. Sound effects of things happening offstage give the impression of a complete world and the audience can imagine the events taking place that they can't see. You can also use the element of surprise with sound, making the audience jump with a sudden loud noise, like a gunshot or thunder.

MAKE-UP (INCLUDING HAIR DESIGN)

Like costume, make-up gives instant clues to character, time period and status. **Naturalistic** make-up and hair can help us read a character and can contribute to audience understanding of character. Other-worldly make-up and hair can create a magical effect. Hair design and wigs can help encourage the audience to believe in characters.

PROPERTIES

The props you use can help to create the desired mood and atmosphere of the show. They can either reinforce the naturalistic setting of a play by fitting perfectly with the style and period, or add to comedy or discomfort and confusion in a **surreal** or **absurdist** play by appearing out of place. You can use many of the same prop to create quite a stylised visual effect, like loads of umbrellas, or use props as symbols, like a flower to represent love.

Personal props also provide the audience with clues about character, location and time period. For example, a mobile phone suggests a contemporary time period in the modern age, or a teddy bear can suggest the age of a character.

SET DESIGN

The design of the set is a major contributor to the mood and atmosphere of a production. You can create an illusion of reality by having an elaborate and realistic looking set or have a more **abstract** and minimal set.

A minimal set can be just as convincing if cleverly designed, but the audience will require imagination to fill in the details of location.

Colours and shapes in your set can be comfortable or uncomfortable depending on their use. For example, the sharp and distorted shapes of **German expressionist** set design deliberately create an uncomfortable atmosphere.

STAGING

The way you choose to stage your production has an effect on mood and atmosphere and you should consider this early on in your plans. If you would like to create an intimate or informal atmosphere where the audience feel involved in the action, or will feel comfortable participating, consider using an **in the round** or **promenade** form. These types don't lend themselves to elaborate sets and scenery, however, so if you want to create a naturalistic effect then you could choose a **proscenium arch** or a **thrust stage**.

DON'T FORGET

Mood and atmosphere contribute to the dramatic **tension** of your production. This is what keeps the audience interested and makes them want to know what's going to happen next.

ONLINE

There are some more ideas for creating mood and atmosphere at www.brightredbooks.net/N5Drama

ONLINE TEST

Take the test on 'Mood and atmosphere' at www.brightredbooks.net/N5Drama

THINGS TO DO AND THINK ABOUT

Try this simple activity to practise setting mood with lighting and music. You will need a box of various personal props at the edge of a performance space, different types of mood music and someone operating the lighting desk. The lighting and sound technicians can choose music and lighting cues as they wish – it doesn't matter if they match.

As soon as the performance space is lit and there is sound, two actors must enter the space and improvise, through mime, an appropriate scene to match the mood created. They can choose appropriate props from the box.

Discuss the effect created by the music and lights, and why the actors made the choices they did after each scene.

GENERATING IDEAS

Generating ideas for a production will be a team effort on the National 5 course. Every production you see or are part of is the result of teamwork: it's a collaborative process involving the ideas of many different people coming together. This takes practice, so every time you have an opportunity to play a part in the decision-making process and to contribute ideas, you should take it.

CREATING A DESIGN CONCEPT

The first thing you need to do as a team is to create a design or directorial concept. If you have an overarching concept, it will give you a direction for directorial decisions and a map for the design of the production. Whenever you are not sure if something fits or you feel you have lost your way creatively, you can come back to the design concept.

It is a good idea to agree this as a team and then everyone will be working to the same idea, even if they are working independently for some of the time. It should also help to ensure that all the elements – acting, lighting, set and so on – come together to create a unified show with a clear vision.

Try to think of one word and one image that capture the design concept for the production. This will contribute to the design brief and will provide a guiding theme for the production, while allowing for creativity and interpretation. Everything that goes into the production should contribute to answering the brief.

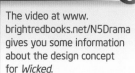

VIDEO LINK

The video at www.
brightredbooks.net/N5Drama
gives you some information
about the design concept
for *Wicked*.

Finale of *The Lion King*

Cogs from *Wicked*

HOW TO FORM A CONCEPT

DEFINE THE PROBLEM

DON'T FORGET

These examples are to
show great design concepts.
Musicals cannot be used for
your Performance in National
5 Drama.

Creating a design concept is a bit like solving a problem, so the first thing you have to do is define what the problem is. In theatre, that usually comes down to: 'what is the aim for the audience experience?' This will come from working with your **text** or **stimulus**. The activities in the 'Generating ideas' (pp 14–15) and 'Selecting ideas' (pp 28–29) sections should help you narrow this down and decide together what themes you want to focus on and emphasise.

contd

RESEARCH

The next step is to do some thorough research. Make sure you know your text really well and research the time period or theme involved. You can also research what others have done with the same text or similar themes to help you generate your own ideas. Have a look at the 'Research skills' (pp 16–17) and 'Research' (pp 62–63) sections for more ideas.

GATHER INSPIRATION

Theatre is a visual medium, so look for visual inspiration. Look at art, nature, architecture, movies, music, stories and magazines for images and ideas that relate to your overall themes or aims.

Create shared mood boards where you can gather images, textures, colours and shapes that could contribute towards the themes and audience experience you are aiming for.

REFINE THE CONCEPT VERBALLY

Try to capture in a word or a phrase the essence of your design concept. Brainstorm individual words or well-known phrases or quotes that come to mind when you look at your mood board. Look for those that sum up the overall impression most effectively. Try to agree on several that best describe the feeling or effect.

REFINE THE CONCEPT VISUALLY

Try also to condense the concept into an image or images to go with your word or phrase. This image should evoke an impression or a feel that you would like to create with the production. It might be a sketch, painting or a photograph that you have found, or have created yourselves.

NEXT STEPS

Once you have decided on a design concept, the creative team can start working on their individual areas and generating ideas for each one. Every role in the production team, including that of the actors, has a responsibility to keep the design concept in mind during the process of production and rehearsals.

Everyone will need to do the research that relates to their role, come up with ideas for how to incorporate the design concept in their area of production and present their ideas to the rest of the team.

VIDEO LINK

The video at www.brightredbooks.net/N5Drama demonstrates how a team works together to contribute to a design concept.

THINGS TO DO AND THINK ABOUT

When creating mood boards, think carefully about the elements you collect. There should be a reason, link or connection between all the ideas so it's not too random.

When giving a presentation about your ideas for your own role (whether that is lighting, costumes or whatever) you should refer back to the design concept and demonstrate how your designs fit the concept and create the right mood and atmosphere.

DON'T FORGET

Record the process of arriving at a design concept in your support log. Include any problems you encountered and the solutions you found for them.

ONLINE TEST

Take the 'Generating Ideas' test at www.brightredbooks.net/N5Drama

RESEARCH

Having an in-depth knowledge and understanding of your theme helps with so many aspects of developing drama. The more you know, the better! This comes from effective and organised research. This section and the 'Research skills' section (pp 16–17) should help with ideas about how to organise your research, what to look for and where to look for information.

START WITH THE TEXT

During this unit, you will be working from an extract of a text, so this is your starting point for research. Whatever your role in the production, you should read the extract carefully and make notes on any clues that are given in the production notes and script. Look for information about time of day, historical period, requirements of the set such as entrances and exits and props, special effects or sound effects required.

If we use *Blood Brothers* by Willy Russell as an example, we can look at the kind of things you might need to research for each production role.

PRODUCTION ROLES

ACTING

If you have an acting role, you will need to research the major themes, the location and the historical context of your play. Make sure you know how your character might speak and behave according to the time period and their status and age.

If it is based on a real life incident or character, make sure you know as much as possible about them. In *Blood Brothers* for example, the setting is 1960s Liverpool, so it would be useful to have some background knowledge about what it might have been like to live in that city around that time. The class system, and the different ways it affects living conditions and opportunities for the working class and middle class, is an important theme in the play, so an insight into that would also be useful.

COSTUME

If you are taking responsibility for costumes in a production, you will need to look in detail at the historical period and setting of the play. Clothing fashions change over time and vary from place to place. To keep costumes authentic, you will need to research the fabrics that were used, and source cheap and practical alternatives. *Blood Brothers* spans a long period from the 1960s to 1980s and the main characters change in age and status throughout the play, so you would need to research what a character of that age would wear in each of the time periods.

LIGHTS

For lighting, most of your research will come from the text. You will need to note locations and times of day throughout the play, so you can design lighting accordingly. You might also want to research techniques for achieving certain effects such as daylight or moonlight to give you some ideas. And although it's not a requirement for National 5, you could include multimedia techniques that involve sourcing film or images to project. It is always useful to look at how someone else has done the same production (or something similar), so watch videos and look at images of previous productions.

SET

If you are designing a set for the production, you will have to ensure that you know the basic functional requirements of the set. How many exits and entrances does it need and how many different settings does it have to represent? You will then need to be

contd

aware of the historical period and location. Certain eras have very distinctive styles in terms of interiors and certain locations have very distinctive architecture. You might need to include local landmarks and references in your set, so videos and images will be a very useful resource.

PROPS

With props, it is very important to check for historical accuracy. For example, if digital clocks haven't yet been invented at the time your play is set, then don't use them on stage. Research, for example, the types of toys children played with, tools people used or possibly items people might have had in the home like telephones, vases and so on.

MAKE-UP AND HAIR

Research how people wore their hair in the time period of your play and what the fashion for make-up was. For example, *Blood Brothers* takes place over a long time period and involves the characters maturing throughout the play, so their hairstyles not only have to illustrate their advancing age but also to reflect the changing fashions through the 1960s, 1970s and 1980s.

There are many images available online of hair and make-up from different eras, and there are even YouTube tutorials that will teach you how to achieve the style.

SOUND

Musical fashions also change over time. You can evoke a time period very effectively by choosing popular music from the time so make sure you research the musical style of the period. *Blood Brothers* spans a time period that includes many iconic and well-known bands and songs that could be used to set the scene. If you're not sure what these are, look them up online or ask someone who will remember!

THINGS TO DO AND THINK ABOUT

As you are researching, make notes in your support log and include images and sketches of your ideas as they develop. You can also include fabric samples, colours, ideas for materials and sound clips.

You should also collect a bibliography of sources as you go. Have a look at the 'Recording evidence – support log' sections (pp 64–65 and 90–91) for more ideas about what to record, and how to record your ideas.

As well as researching the themes and time periods of the play, think about researching where to source the materials or props you might need. This can sometimes take a great deal of time and it is very useful to have a few ideas up your sleeve for where to go to borrow items of costume, scenery or props. The internet is a great resource for this, but so are the people in your local area!

ONLINE

Andy Walmsley designed the set for the Broadway production of *Blood Bothers*. You can see his models and final designs at www. brightredbooks.net/N5Drama

DON'T FORGET

When you are researching the text, think about problems or difficulties that you might encounter with your area of production. It pays to be prepared, so start thinking about creative solutions early in the process.

DON'T FORGET

Be careful not to copy ideas directly. Taking inspiration is fine, but try to make sure you develop the idea in your own way rather than just reproducing what someone else has done.

ONLINE

If you are staging *Blood Brothers*, there is some useful information at www. brightredbooks.net/N5Drama to help with research.

ONLINE TEST

Take the 'Research' test at www.brightredbooks.net/N5Drama

RECORDING EVIDENCE

It is important throughout the course that you document your learning as this will help you when you come to the assessment. Here we call this a support log but it can take many forms. This is a very important learning tool and should be your constant companion during your course. Use it to collect ideas and reflect on rehearsals and designs.

THINGS TO INCLUDE

Whether you are acting or designing the lighting, sound or costumes, you should follow a similar process for recording evidence. The format will probably differ because some will include drawn designs and some might include video of rehearsals, but you still need to record something about each of the areas below.

NOTES ON SCRIPT OR STIMULUS

Start off by recording or gathering all your notes and evidence on the script or stimulus. This should include how it was chosen and whether you were part of that decision-making process. You should make notes on every discussion that your group has made about this in the planning stages and include ideas that were discarded along the way, with the reasons why. You can include extracts of script in your support log as evidence if you have actually made notes on the script.

IDENTIFICATION OF REQUIREMENTS

Identify your requirements: this means listing the responsibilities of your role, what they require you to do and what their implications are. At this initial stage, you will only be using the script to help you, because you won't yet have decided on a design concept.

For example, if you are designing the set, you might note that you need to represent an interior scene and a street scene on the stage at the same time, with three different exits and entrances.

If you are designing the costume, you might note that you need a certain number of costumes.

If you are designing lights, you might note the interior and exterior scenes, times of day and any special effects required.

DESIGN CONCEPT

Record the process of deciding on the **design concept** for the production. This will include notes about your discussions with the director, fellow designers and the cast to agree on a design concept that will guide your design decisions.

Remember to include ideas that were discarded, the reasons why and any problems that you encountered during the process.

RESEARCH

Keep a record of all your research. Make notes on what you decided to research, how you researched it and what you discovered. At the end of the research process, try to summarise the key things that you think will be relevant to your designs and to the production.

PREPARATION OF DESIGN

For each area of production, make notes on your initial ideas for the production. You should include your ideal designs and then make modifications to take account of what you actually have available to use. This should include **lighting charts**, **cue sheets** for sound, **plan drawings** of set, photographs of make-up trials or final costume design sketches.

contd

PREPARATION/ORGANISATION OF MATERIALS

You will need to identify what you have available to you and record any problems and solutions with sourcing or affording materials. List everything you already have along with the things you might need to make or borrow. If you are borrowing equipment, record every item and where it has been borrowed from.

NOTES ON REHEARSALS

Make notes on all the rehearsals that you attend. Include what you did, what the difficulties were and what solutions were found.

For the **technical** and **dress rehearsal**, write how it went, what did and didn't work and how you might change that. Each time, try to include an aim for the next rehearsal.

REFINEMENT/ADJUSTMENT

This section is about reflection. Look back at the rehearsals and try to assess how effective your ideas and designs were. Now that you have seen how they might work in the performance, consider possible solutions to issues that have arisen during rehearsals or ways to improve on your initial ideas.

PERFORMANCE

Keep a record, too, of how the performance goes. If you have been in the audience or backstage operating lights or sound, reflect on that experience. Comment on the positives as well as problems that arose. Consider how having an audience changed things and remember to justify your opinions.

Include audience comments about the performance in your support log.

Think about how you would improve things next time if you were to do it again.

REMOVAL/STORAGE/RESET

For most production roles, there will be responsibilities and work to do after the performance to prepare for the following night or to organise and store all the materials once all performances have finished. For example, you might need to **strike** the set, store the costumes, make-up and wigs or reset sound and lighting equipment.

You should record your strategy for doing this to demonstrate that you have thought about the issues involved with organisation and storage. For example, if you have a costume store, all of the costumes you have used will need to be wrapped as necessary and returned to their proper place so they can be found for future performances. You might even need to design a system for organising the store as part of your job.

You might have to borrow some of your lighting and sound equipment specifically for the performance. If this is the case, you will need to dismantle it and organise for it to be returned to the owner. Make notes about how you have done this and any problems you have encountered.

DON'T FORGET

You must always think about **why** in your support log. Why have you made that decision? Why did you discard that idea? Why did it work well?

THINGS TO DO AND THINK ABOUT

If you decide to store all your evidence electronically, try to back it up and store it in at least two places: that way your work will not be lost if the system crashes.

You could collect feedback from your audience by designing a questionnaire and putting one copy on each seat before the performance. That way you can ask specific questions about the set, costumes, acting and so on. (Don't make it too long, or people won't fill it in.)

Alternatively, you could ask someone from another group – or perhaps a student from a media studies class – to interview and film some audience members as they are leaving, in best movie premier style. They could ask the audience what they thought of the show, what they thought the best bit was and any areas that they thought could be improved.

ONLINE

Have a look at the online organiser at www.brightredbooks.net/N5Drama for a new way to record evidence.

ONLINE TEST

Take the test on recording evidence at www.brightredbooks.net/N5Drama

STAGING

You need to decide early on in the rehearsal process how you are going to stage your performance. Are you going to stage it **in the round**, on a **proscenium arch** stage, outside or perhaps on a **traverse stage**? This decision will affect many areas of the production, so you will need to make it before you get too far down the line. One of the key factors to consider is the space you have available to you at school or college – it might have limitations, so bear this in mind when creating your production.

TYPES OF STAGING

Staging is the position of the acting area relative to the audience. Every stage is different in terms of size, shape, acoustics, backstage areas and atmosphere.

There are many ways to stage a performance, but the standard ones are listed below.

PROSCENIUM ARCH OR END ON

A **proscenium arch** or **end on stage** is perhaps the most common and traditional form of stage, and what you would expect in most theatres. The audience all sit in front of a raised stage with an arch around it. It gives the impression of there being a **fourth wall** between the actors and audience which creates a bit of distance between them.

This type of staging is quite easy to use as there is generally a large backstage area, and the fact that the audience sit on one side makes for straightforward **blocking** and sight lines. Things to remember about this type of stage are that sound can get lost if not projected and directed beyond the arch, and that the distance between the audience and the performers means the audience can feel removed from the action.

IN THE ROUND

Theatre in the round means that there is audience on all sides of the acting area. This can create a very intimate atmosphere, because the audience are usually very close to the action and feel quite involved.

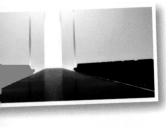

Audience participation works well with theatre in the round.

Challenges with this type of staging are that you have to be very careful with blocking to make sure that all members of the audience get a good view of what's going on. You also have to use a minimal set so you don't block any sight lines.

TRAVERSE STAGE

A traverse stage is sometimes also called an avenue or corridor stage. It involves the audience sitting on either side of the performance area, facing each other. The audience are close to the action, and feel involved in it, so this therefore creates an intimate atmosphere.

This type of staging works well for a production involving lots of movement or travelling because the 'avenue' arrangement implies and encourages movement along it.

Challenges include making sure that both sides of the audience can see and hear at all times and that the space is lit so as not to cast shadows on one side.

Like theatre in the round, a traverse stage usually has a minimal set so as not to block sight lines.

THRUST

A thrust stage is also a common arrangement and can take different forms in itself.

Some thrust stages look almost like a proscenium arch, but have a protrusion at the front so that most of the audience are end on, with a few seated on the sides.

Others are almost in the round, but have the audience on three sides only like the well-known Globe Theatre in London.

PROMENADE THEATRE

Promenade theatre is very different from the rest, in that the audience moves around and the acting area could be anything or anywhere. It might all happen over the audience's heads, in different rooms of a building or in a variety of locations outside.

This type of staging is probably the most intimate for the audience, because they actually have to participate by moving around.

contd

AREAS OF A THEATRE

These are the main areas of a traditional theatre:

Apron – a part of the stage that protrudes into the auditorium.

Auditorium – this is the part of the theatre where the audience sits.

Fly tower – a space above the stage that is out of sight of the audience. Elements of scenery can be flown onto the stage from here.

Front of House – the part of the theatre open to the public before they reach the auditorium.

House curtain – the curtain at the front of a proscenium arch stage.

Offstage – the area backstage, away from the performance area.

Onstage – the performance area visible to the audience.

Trap – a trap door in the floor of the stage.

Wings – the offstage areas at the sides of the stage.

THE ACTING AREA/AREAS OF THE STAGE

It is important for all members of the production team and cast to understand the acting area and how this translates to stage directions. The acting area is that part of the stage occupied by the set and used by the actors when acting.

There are nine areas of the stage and they are named from the perspective of the actors facing out towards the audience:

- Up Stage Right (USR)
- Up Stage Centre (USC)
- Up Stage Left (USL)
- Centre Stage Right (CSR)
- Centre Stage (CS)
- Centre Stage Left (CSL)
- Down Stage Right (DSR)
- Down Stage Centre (DSC)
- Down Stage Left (DSL)

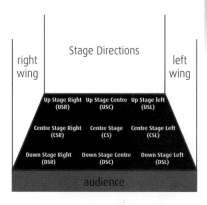

OTHER STAGING ELEMENTS

RAKE

Some stages are **raked**, meaning that they slope downwards towards the audience. This helps with the visibility of performers towards the back of the stage, and can help if you have many people on stage at once.

REVOLVING STAGE

If you are very lucky, you might have access to a revolving stage. These are platforms that are put onto the stage and can be rotated either manually or mechanically to aid quick scene changes or to portray travelling.

RAISED AREA

This refers to a platform that could either form the entire stage or a part of the stage. This can be useful for creating a split stage to portray different locations and times.

THINGS TO DO AND THINK ABOUT

If you have no stage and are using a classroom or studio, you will need to think about how you will manage this. Do you want a backstage area or do you want the audience to see everything?

There are ways to create a backstage area out of sight of the audience using elements of scenery, such as stage flats or curtains. You could also use a separate room as a **green room** if there is one available.

DON'T FORGET

Make sure that you document your decision-making process about staging in your support log. Mention what your options were, what you have chosen and the reasons why.

ONLINE

There is some useful information about staging at www.brightredbooks.net/N5Drama

ONLINE TEST

What have you learned about staging? Take the test at www.brightredbooks.net/N5Drama

SET

In theatre, the **set** is the scenery and furniture in the acting area that indicates the setting of a play. The set designer researches and plans – and often makes – the whole set for a production. If you are responsible for designing a set for your production, you might not have to make it, but your design choices should reflect the ideas and themes of the play.

ONLINE

There are some useful resources about set design at www.brightredbooks.net/N5Drama

Black Watch set

DON'T FORGET

Make sure that you are aware of health and safety considerations in set design and building. See the section on 'Health and Safety' (pp 82–83) for more information about this.

RESPONSIBILITIES OF THE SET DESIGNER

READ THE SCRIPT

Start by reading the script, or extract, several times. Read through once to make sure you know the story and themes of the play. Then start reading again and mark up your script to highlight any information and stage directions about the set. You will get many clues about the various settings of the play, the period the play is set in and practical elements like entrances and exits from a close reading of the script.

WORK WITH THE TEAM

You will need to work closely with the rest of the production team, since many aspects of your role will impact on theirs. You should have regular discussions about the interpretation of the text with the director, lighting designer, props manager, costume designer and cast.

The lighting designer will also advise you about aspects of lighting on the set such as where to create shadows and where to avoid them.

RESEARCH

Once you know the extract well and have settled on themes and a concept for your production, you should research the style, period, setting and atmosphere. It is vital that you have good background knowledge so your design reflects the setting effectively and creates the desired atmosphere.

You will also need to research practical aspects so you are aware of any limitations you have to deal with. Consider the size and nature of your stage or performance area and any restrictions such as **sight lines**.

MAKE DESIGN DECISIONS

As the set designer, your creative decisions have to reflect the **design concept** that the team has decided upon, whether that involves an elaborate, **naturalistic** set or a more **stylised** and **abstract** one.

If your resources are limited, you will need to be very creative about how you represent the setting with minimal scenery. The National Theatre of Scotland's *Black Watch* is a very good example of a minimal set where a pool table and scaffolding are used in various ways to represent different elements of set. You can also use projections creatively to create backgrounds and scenery without expensive materials.

PRODUCE A GROUND PLAN AND ELEVATION

During the process of designing the set, you will do many draft drawings and working designs, but it is important that you produce a final **ground plan** of the set showing where everything will be on the stage. If possible, you should draw this roughly to scale or at least indicate measurements. Mark out the stage to make sure that everything will fit.

You should also produce an **elevation** drawing of your design.

SOURCE MATERIALS AND BUILD

You will be responsible for sourcing materials, taking health and safety regulations into consideration and ensuring that the set can be moved as required. There will be limits

contd

to what you can build yourself, so you might need help. If someone else is building the set, you must oversee this and ensure that it is suitable.

REFINE AND ADJUST

There will often be decisions made in rehearsals that will result in an adjustment to the set. It is important that you attend rehearsals to make note of these changes and adapt your design accordingly. Keep a rehearsal diary to note any problems and possible solutions.

STRIKE THE SET

After the performance, it is your responsibility to dismantle and store the set. You might need to reset the stage to a neutral state and return any items that have been borrowed.

DON'T FORGET

Everything you do during the process of designing the set should be documented in your support log because it will play a big part in your final examination. Record it all – it's important.

KEY TERMS AND VOCABULARY

Backcloth – a large cloth – either painted or black – that hangs at the back of the stage.

Bar – a metal bar that sits horizontally above the stage for suspending lights, cloths, and other items of scenery.

Cloth – a hanging cloth that can be painted as part of the set.

Cyclorama – a large curtain, wall or screen – sometimes concave and usually white – at the back of the stage.

Entrance – a place onstage or within the set where a performer can enter the acting area.

Exit – a place onstage or within the set where a performer can leave the acting area.

Flat – a flat piece of scenery that can be freestanding or suspended. These can be painted to form part of the scenery or set.

Fly system – a system that allows you to hoist elements of scenery upwards into the **fly** above the stage.

Marking – marks on the stage, usually made with tape, that indicate the positions of set and props.

Split stage – this type of stage has two or more areas that depict different locations or times. It allows you to change the location or time without a complete set or scenery change.

Strike – to strike the set means to remove, dismantle and store the set and scenery after a performance.

Tabs – curtains that hang at the sides of the stage to obscure the **wings**. They can also be a pair of curtains that meet in the middle of the stage and overlap. The **house curtain** is sometimes called **front tabs**.

DRAWING A GROUND PLAN

You will need to produce a ground plan for your set. A ground plan is a bird's-eye view of the set, showing furniture, entrances/exits and the position of the audience. You can draw this by hand or, alternatively, use a drawing or computer-aided design programme such as 'Stage Write' – an iPad app.

It is important that your ground plan shows:
- delineation of the stage
- the position of the audience
- entrances/exits
- set marked on stage
- a key of symbols used

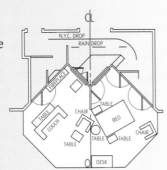

KEY SYMBOLS

Below are some suggested symbols for elements of set and scenery. You can design symbols for any other items that you might use, but these should be clearly explained in the key so other people can read your plan.

Plain flat	Rostrum
Door flat	Stairs/Treads
Window flat	Curtain
Chair	Lamp
Sofa	
Table	

THINGS TO DO AND THINK ABOUT

Mark out the elements of scenery and set in the performance area with tape. This will help you to imagine things in place and visualise whether they will fit and allow space for movement.

ONLINE TEST

What have you learned about sets? Take the test at www. brightredbooks.net/N5Drama

LIGHTING

If your school or college has a lighting rig consisting of a minimum of eight lanterns of various types (including **flood**, **Fresnel** and **profile spots**), you could take on the role of lighting designer for a production. This role involves both creativity and technical expertise.

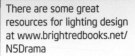

ONLINE

There are some great resources for lighting design at www.brightredbooks.net/N5Drama

ONLINE

There is some useful information about how to create grid plans and channel lists at www.brightredbooks.net/N5Drama

DON'T FORGET

The lighting rig available for use in this production role must consist of a minimum of eight lanterns.

RESPONSIBILITIES OF A LIGHTING DESIGNER

READ THE SCRIPT

Start by reading the script, or extract, several times. Read through once to make sure you know the story and themes of the play. Then start reading again and mark up your script to highlight any information and stage directions about the lighting. You will get many clues about the various settings of the play, the period the play is set in and practical elements like entrances and exits from a close reading of the script.

WORK WITH THE TEAM

You will need to work in collaboration with the director, set designer, sound manager, costume designer, make-up designer and cast because what you do will affect what they do.

It is particularly important that you liaise with the set designer to discuss which elements will be included on set, and where they will be, so you can light them accordingly. You also need to collaborate to ensure that there are no unwanted shadows or reflections on stage.

RESEARCH

Do some background research about the time period and setting of the play. For example, you need to know if there were only oil lamps available for lighting during that period, so you can replicate a suitably authentic effect and atmosphere.

Research and assess the performance area and the equipment you have available to you, so you are aware of any limitations they might impose.

MAKE DESIGN DECISIONS

As the lighting designer, your creative decisions about lighting have to reflect the **design concept** that the team has decided upon. You need to choose the type of lights, the effects and colours and any **special effects** that will reflect the time and place of the action.

You could present your initial ideas to the rest of the design team to ensure that you are reflecting the ideas and themes of the play, and creating the appropriate mood and atmosphere. Keep this discussion going throughout rehearsals.

CREATE A LIGHTING PLOT AND CUE SHEET

You will need to produce a **lighting plot** or **grid plan** for the performance. This is a diagram showing the positions of the lights you are using in your venue. You can draw this by hand or on a computer.

You could also create a **master channel list**. This is basically a numbered list of all the lanterns being used, with any additional information about **gobos** and **gels** attached. For your assessment, you will need to design a minimum of five **lighting states** and have seven or more lighting cues.

For the performance, you will also need a **cue sheet**. This tells you the cue for each lighting change in the script, and the strength and speed of the fade along with any information about special effects.

contd

PREPARE THE LIGHTING

It is your responsibility to prepare the lighting for the show. This will involve rigging and focusing the lights according to your design, or perhaps advising and instructing a technician to do this on your behalf.

REFINE AND ADJUST

There will often be decisions made in rehearsals that will result in an adjustment to the lighting. It is important that you attend rehearsals to make note of these changes and adapt your lighting design accordingly. Keep a rehearsal diary to note any problems and possible solutions.

The technical rehearsal will be particularly important for you, because this is when you will make any final adjustments and test everything before the performance.

PERFORM

It will be a major part of your job to operate the lights during the performances. To avoid any unforeseen complications, be prepared! Flash through the lights before each performance to check the lamps and the focusing. Have spare bulbs available and have a back-up plan in case something goes wrong.

STRIKE THE LIGHTING RIG

After the last performance, it might be your responsibility to reset all the lights to a default arrangement and to dismantle and return any borrowed equipment.

DON'T FORGET

You must document the process of designing lighting for a production in your support log. Include your marked-up script, research, design ideas, grid plans and information about problems and solutions.

DON'T FORGET

Make sure that you are aware of health and safety issues that relate to lighting design. Have a look at the section about Health and Safety (pp 82–83) for more information about this.

KEY TERMS AND VOCABULARY

Barn doors – shutters mounted on the front of a lantern to enable you to shape and direct the light.

Blackout – when all the lights are extinguished on stage. This can either be a slow fade blackout or a sudden blackout, and blackouts are often used to indicate the passage of time or the end of a scene.

Crossfade – when one lighting cue fades into another without a blackout in between.

Fast fade – when lighting fades out quickly.

Flood – a type of lantern that gives a wide, bright spread of light.

Focusing – when the lanterns are directed at the correct place and angle to achieve the desired effect.

Follow spot – a powerful and bright beam of light that can follow actors around the stage.

Fresnel Spot – a type of lantern that produces a soft-edged beam of light.

G clamp – a clamp used to fix a lantern to a bar or a stand.

Gel – a coloured filter applied to a lantern to change the colour of the light.

Gobo – a metal plate with a design cut into it that goes in front of a lantern to project an image or an effect onto the performance area.

LFX – an abbreviated term for lighting effects.

Lighting desk – a control desk or board for the lighting.

Profile spot – a type of lantern that gives a hard-edged beam of light.

Rigging – the structure that lights hang from in a theatre, or the activity of hanging lights.

Safety chain – a chain that goes around the lantern and bar to provide extra safety.

Slow fade – when lighting is faded out slowly.

Special effects – lighting effects such as a strobe, lightning or a camera flash.

T-Bar – a floor-stand onto which lanterns can be attached.

Wash – lighting the whole stage evenly.

THINGS TO DO AND THINK ABOUT

Ask a friend or a cast member to stand in the performance area and experiment with different lighting techniques. Try lighting them from above and below, creating shadows and using strobe effects. Try using different colours and gobos. Take photographs or make notes about what works well for certain moods and effects.

ONLINE TEST

Head to www. brightredbooks.net/N5Drama and take the test on lighting!

SOUND

As a sound designer, your responsibilities range from choosing music and sound effects, amplification of voices and controlling volume levels to ensuring that everything can be heard perfectly. Like the lighting designer, you need to combine creativity and technical skills to enhance the mood and atmosphere of a production.

RESPONSIBILITIES OF THE SOUND DESIGNER

READ THE SCRIPT

As with all the production roles, your job as sound designer starts with reading the script or extract through several times so you know the story and are aware of the content, style, period, atmosphere and setting of the play. Note down requirements and ideas for sound effects and music. Stage directions such as 'a loud crash is heard' or 'he exits slamming the door' will also give you some ideas.

WORK WITH THE TEAM

You are a member of a team, so you must therefore discuss the sound effects requirements with the director, other production team members and the cast. The sound must be coordinated with the action, so you need to organise sound and music during rehearsals to help the actors know their cues.

RESEARCH

Research the period and location of the play. You might need to know about music from a specific country or era and how to produce certain sound effects to create an authentic setting and atmosphere for the production.

You might also need to research where to source sound effects, how to create them, how to record voice-overs and how to find music requested by the director.

MAKE DESIGN DECISIONS

As the sound designer, your creative decisions about sounds and music have to reflect the **design concept** that the team has decided upon. You need to source the sound effects and music and complete a sound **cue sheet** showing pre-show and incidental music, sound effects, the source of sound, the volume and duration of each sound.

PREPARE EQUIPMENT

It is your job to ensure that you have all the equipment you need – including a mixing desk, microphones and computer software – and that you know how to use it. If you are borrowing equipment for a production, organise how it will be picked up and dropped off.

Create a playlist or load sounds onto the programme or equipment you are using, so that there is no delay before the sound plays.

There is a great deal of sound software available to experiment with, and much of it is free.

REFINE AND ADJUST

It is very important that you attend rehearsals and practise operating the sound several times before the performance because you will probably need to resolve issues and make adjustments to sound levels and durations.

Work closely with the cast so everyone knows how to respond to cues. Keep a rehearsal diary to note things you might need to change or problems you need to solve.

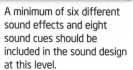

DON'T FORGET

A minimum of six different sound effects and eight sound cues should be included in the sound design at this level.

ONLINE

Head to www.brightredbooks. net to find links for free sound production and cue softwares Multiplay and Audacity.

contd

PERFORM

One of the most important aspects of your role will be to operate the sound during the performance. For this you will need to use a cue sheet, check all the equipment is working and perform a sound check to test for volume levels before the performance.

AFTER THE SHOW

Once all the performances are over, you will be responsible for dismantling and returning any borrowed equipment and resetting or storing the sound equipment.

ONLINE

There is some useful information about sound design at www.brightredbooks.net/N5Drama

DON'T FORGET

You must document the whole process of sound design for a production in your support log. Make sure you include design ideas, any problems you encountered and how you solved the problems.

DON'T FORGET

Make sure you are aware of any health and safety considerations involved in sound design. See the section about health and safety (pp 82–83) for more help and information about this.

KEY TERMS AND VOCABULARY

Crossfade – when one sound is faded out and another faded in with no break in between.

Cue – a signal for a sound effect to begin or end.

Fade in – bringing a sound in by slowly increasing the volume.

Fade out – slowly decreasing the volume of a sound until it stops.

Live SFX – a sound effect that is created live during the performance.

Mixing desk – a control desk for sound effects, microphones and music.

Pre-recorded SFX – a sound effect or music that has been recorded prior to the performance.

THINGS TO DO AND THINK ABOUT

Remember that not every sound has to be produced electronically. There is still a place for live sound. Can you use physical objects or people to create sounds such as crashes or gunshots off stage?

ONLINE TEST

How well have you learned this topic? Head to www.brightredbooks.net/N5Drama to take the test.

PROPERTIES

If you are responsible for the props for a show, your title is properties (props) manager. There is some overlap with this role and that of the set and costume designers, so you will need to work closely with those members of the team.

Your role is particularly important if there is minimal set and costume being used in the production, because you might have to suggest location or character with one carefully chosen prop.

RESPONSIBILITIES OF THE PROPERTIES MANAGER

READ THE SCRIPT

Get to know the extract or script well. Read it first to understand the story and then study it in greater detail to find out what props are needed. There might, for example, be a stage direction such as 'he takes a gun from the drawer' that tells you which prop is needed and where it needs to be placed on the stage.

The script will contain many clues like this and you need to note them all.

MAKE A PROPS LIST

After you have read the script, make a preliminary props list. This will inevitably change as you go through the rehearsal process and more detailed requirements become clear.

Eventually you will be able to create a **master props list** including all the **personal props**, **set props** and **costume props** required. You should include information about each prop including what it is, where it is at the beginning of the show, where it is at the end of the show, who uses it and any maintenance information.

WORK WITH THE TEAM

Liaise with other members of your group to make sure that the props list is complete and that all props are appropriate for the style and mood of the play.

The style of props you choose should reflect the **design concept** that the team has agreed upon. You should also consult the director about your choice.

You need to work closely with the actors using the props so that they don't experience any difficulties. For example, if an actor has to use a sword, make sure that it's not too heavy or long for them to wield comfortably.

It is also important that you work closely with the set designer on **set dressing** and the costume designer on **costume props** to ensure that the style and the characters are represented consistently.

RESEARCH

You will need to do some research on periods, style and setting for your production to make sure your props are appropriate and in keeping with the mood and atmosphere of the play. Look at images and videos of previous productions of the same play or productions in a similar style for ideas.

SOURCE PROPS

As properties manager, it is your responsibility to source all the props required for the performance and to note where they have come from. You might find some items in your props store, but you'll probably have to borrow or make others.

Practise making props – you are required to make one for your final assessment.

Label any items that you have borrowed so you return them to the correct people. Don't borrow anything that is irreplaceable, breakable or expensive!

contd

PROPS TABLE

A central aspect of your job as props manager is to create and keep a **props table**. This is a table backstage where all the props are stored. This should be organised so that you know exactly where everything goes and easily accessible for everyone who needs to use it.

Brief actors on your system so they can easily find the props they need and know where to return them. Start this process early in rehearsals: it can be very distracting in a performance if you have a new prop that you have never used before.

Be aware that there could be other groups using the performance space as well as you – so store all the props safely in between rehearsals.

PERFORM

During the performance you might be backstage helping with scene changes. Check before, after and during performances that all props are where they should be.

MAINTENANCE AND REPAIR

Props can become damaged during rehearsals and performances, and it is your job to repair them. Check all the props regularly for damage and have resources such as glue, tape and string handy for quick repairs backstage.

STORE

After the performance, you will be responsible for returning borrowed props and storing others. Labelling each prop so that you know where it comes from makes this process much simpler.

An inventory of your props store is also useful.

KEY TERMS AND VOCABULARY

Costume props – these are items that form part of a costume that an actor wears, but the props manager takes responsibility for them rather than the costume designer. These might include things like hats, glasses, armour and weapons.

Master props list – the list of all props and any information about how they are used in the show.

Personal props – These are props – like a wallet or a walking stick – that are carried by the actor. Personal props are usually issued to an actor rather than stored on the props table, and the actor is responsible for them.

Set props – this is a prop placed on the set – like a gun in the drawer – or a prop that forms part of the set dressing – like a table lamp or a vase of flowers.

THINGS TO DO AND THINK ABOUT

You could create a checklist for your own use backstage to help scene changes to run smoothly. Write the checklist on a large sheet of paper and list all the props required scene by scene. You can stick this on a wall or on the back of a scenery flat.

DON'T FORGET

You will need to document your job in your support log, remembering to include ideas, inspirations, any problems you encountered and how you solved them.

DON'T FORGET

Make sure you are aware of health and safety issues when working backstage. Have a look at the section on health and safety (pp 82–83) for more advice about this.

ONLINE

Follow the link at www.brightredbooks.net/N5Drama for a really useful website for anyone responsible for managing props.

ONLINE TEST

How well have you learned this topic? Take the test at www.brightredbooks.net/N5Drama

PRODUCTION SKILLS

COSTUME

Costume is essential to a performance, and the role of costume designer is vital to the style, mood and atmosphere of a production. Costume gives clues about characters and themes and creates visual balance on stage. As a costume designer, you will develop an understanding of how clothes communicate with an audience and the practical aspects of how costumes can help or hinder a performance. It is a creative role with some technical aspects including how to construct or adapt clothes.

VIDEO LINK

Head to www. brgithredbooks.net/N5Drama and watch the video about the costume design for *Wicked* which highlights the importance of thinking about characters.

ONLINE

Some very useful costume research websites are the Museum of Costume and the V&A museum – head to www.brightredbooks. net/N5Drama and follow the links!

VIDEO LINK

There is an interesting video about the costume design concept for a modern production of Romeo and Juliet at www.brightredbooks. net/N5Drama

RESPONSIBILITIES OF THE COSTUME DESIGNER

READ THE SCRIPT

Start by reading the script or extract. Read first to understand the story and then re-read to pick up clues about costume from the text. Think about the location and time period and what this means for costume. Will it need to be **period costume** or could you update it?

You will also need to know the characters well, so list all the characters and anything you notice about them that could affect their costume. It might be an aspect of personality that suggests a particular way of dressing or something you want to emphasise about them – for example, vulnerability or confidence.

There are also practical considerations that you should note from reading the script – for example, does the costume need pockets, or does the character need to be active in it?

WORK WITH THE TEAM

Discuss requirements for costume with the director, cast and the rest of the production team. You will need to work closely with the actors as they will have ideas about how to play their character and it's important that they feel the costume fits the character. Having the right costume can really help an actor to identify with and feel like their character. If they feel the costume is wrong this will be difficult. You should also work closely with the make-up and hair designer so the whole look of a character reflects the same style and feel.

RESEARCH

You will need to do some thorough research so you are aware of fashions and styles from the time and the place of the play. You could also research how particular types of people dress and what certain clothes can signify. Think about the assumptions that people make about certain groups of people who have a distinctive look.

DESIGN COSTUMES

As the costume designer, you get to make the creative decisions about what the characters look like. Once you have read the script, make some preliminary sketches that reflect the **design concept** and present your ideas to the team. Your designs should reflect the style and period of the play and be appropriate for each character. All the clothing that is seen on stage should be chosen or designed specifically for the performance.

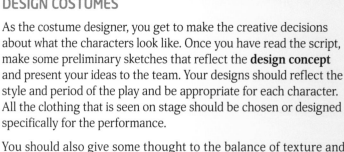

You should also give some thought to the balance of texture and colour on stage in each scene. In the dress rehearsal, notice if anyone stands out when they shouldn't or if some characters are less noticeable because of their costumes. Make a note of any changes you make and the reasons why. You should produce final costume designs and a **costume list** (including undergarments) for every character and use this to create the costumes.

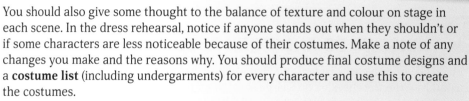

contd

PROVIDE COSTUMES

Once you have created your costume designs, your job is to provide the costumes for all of the characters in the performance. This should include at least one made or adapted costume. You might be lucky enough to have access to a costume store that has costumes you could either use or adapt to fit your designs. The actors themselves might be able to contribute their own clothes or borrow them from friends and family. If you do borrow any clothes, it is vital that you label them carefully so you know who they belong to.

Build in plenty of time for fittings with each of the actors. This will allow you to check that the costume fits and to make any alterations required.

BE ORGANISED

A very important aspect of the costume designer's job is to be organised. It can be hectic backstage, so rack and label all the costumes to keep track of everything. Each character's costume should be on a hanger, labelled with the name of the actor who wears it.

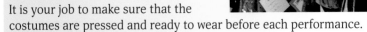

It is your job to make sure that the costumes are pressed and ready to wear before each performance.

PERFORMANCE

Be available backstage during performances to make repairs and help with costume changes. Remember to check that all costumes are present and in good repair before and after performances.

AFTER THE SHOW

Once the performance has finished, it will be your responsibility to return all costumes to the correct place, in the condition that you found them. Carefully wash any clothes that you have borrowed from other people before you return them to the owners. Costumes that are going back into your costume store should be put in the correct place, so they can be easily found the next time they are needed.

KEY TERMS AND VOCABULARY

Costume – clothes worn by performers on stage.

Costume list – a master list of each character and every item of costume they need.

Hats – could either be your responsibility or that of the props manager.

Jewellery – earrings, necklaces, rings and bracelets form part of the costumes and should add to the overall effect.

Masks – an object worn to cover the face.

Period costume – costumes that reflect a particular time period.

Wigs – artificial hair pieces. These need careful maintenance and care.

THINGS TO DO AND THINK ABOUT

If you are interested in costume design, it's really useful to be able to sew. It's easy to learn and very satisfying when you can make something yourself. Start with sewing by hand so you are able to quickly fix a seam, a button or a hem with a few stitches. This will be useful for quick fixes backstage in rehearsals or performances.

VIDEO LINK

There is a great film about the maintenance of theatre costumes at www.brightredbooks.net/N5Drama

DON'T FORGET

Flat black or white costumes don't work particularly well on stage. Black offers little contrast and interest and white reflects under the lights and draws the eye. Try using colours that are subtly different such as navy or cream instead.

DON'T FORGET

Document the process of designing costumes for a production in your support log. Show initial ideas and sketches, inspirations, final designs and evidence of problem-solving.

ONLINE TEST

How well have you learned this topic? Take the test at www.brightredbooks.net/N5Drama

MAKE-UP AND HAIR

As with costume, make-up and hair design communicates a great deal of information to the audience about period, style and character. Audiences watch actors' faces closely so the make-up plays a huge part in making a character believable.

RESPONSIBILITIES OF THE MAKE-UP AND HAIR DESIGNER

READ THE SCRIPT

It is essential that you know the script or extract well because your designs will be based on this. Read it through once to make sure you know the story, and then re-read and make notes on characters and any specific physical marks or characteristics they have – for example, there might be one character who has bruises or a black eye, or another who looks untidy and dishevelled.

Mark up your script to remind yourself of these aspects.

WORK WITH THE TEAM

Discuss the themes of the play and the requirements for each character with other members of the team. You will be working particularly closely with the director, actors and the costume and lighting designers.

Consult the director and costume designer about their ideas for characters, and create your designs in collaboration with the lighting designer: lighting can completely change the look of a face.

Identify and record any allergies that cast members might have to specific make-up and hair products.

RESEARCH

Do some thorough research on the period and style of the play to ensure that your designs are authentic and appropriate. You should also research how different types of people would wear their make-up, as this can vary between social groups.

If you are creating more elaborate looks like animals or aliens, research techniques and different ways to create these creatures. If you are new to stage make-up design, research the types of products that are normally used, and check out health and safety considerations.

DESIGN MAKE-UP AND HAIR

As the make-up and hair designer for a production, you get to design all the looks for the characters. Once you have discussed themes and a **design concept** with the rest of the team, you should create initial hair and make-up designs for all the characters. Present your ideas to the team explaining how the designs reflect the character, status, background and themes of the play. Do some trial runs with the actors and photograph the results. Note any changes and refinements that you need to make.

Complete a chart for any characters that need make-up, including any special make-up effects such as injuries. Have final design drawings or photographs for all the characters ready for the performance.

contd

MAINTAIN MAKE-UP STORE

As part of your role you will be responsible for keeping the make-up store in good order. If make-up is old or past its use-by date, throw it out. Make sure that everything you need is in the kit, and keep it clean and organised.

PERFORMANCE

You will be responsible for applying make-up or overseeing the application of make-up for dress-rehearsals and for the performance. Ensure that it looks effective on stage.

AFTER THE SHOW

After the final performance it is your responsibility to clean, discard and store the make-up appropriately. Wash and dry sponges and brushes before you store them, and close any containers so that the make-up doesn't dry out.

KEY TERMS AND VOCABULARY

Crepe hair – woven strands of artificial hair that can be used for eyebrows, beards and moustaches.

Foundation – base make-up that creates an even colour. Other make-up can be applied on top of this.

Highlighting – a technique of emphasising facial features with light-coloured make-up to catch the light.

Liners – usually make-up pencils in varying colours that achieve a defined line.

Nose putty – a type of wax that you can apply to the face to change the shape of the nose and other facial features. It can also be used for creating scars and warts.

Shading – a technique of emphasising facial features by colouring the hollows of the face with darker make-up.

Skull cap – a flesh-coloured head covering made of plastic to create the effect of being bald.

Spirit gum – an adhesive for attaching false hair and other prosthetics. (Try to get a water soluble variety.)

Stage blood – artificial blood. (Try to get a variety that doesn't stain.)

Stipple sponge – a textured make-up sponge that can create certain effects like stubble and broken veins.

Tooth wax – blackout wax that can be applied to a tooth to make it appear as if it's missing.

THINGS TO DO AND THINK ABOUT

Stage lighting tends to flatten a face, so an important skill to learn is how to highlight the features of the actors to combat this effect. Experiment with highlighting and shading techniques and look at the effect under the stage lights. Take photographs of your experiments and note what worked well and which techniques you need to practice.

ONLINE

Some useful tips on make-up can be found at www.brightredbooks.net/N5Drama

DON'T FORGET

You will need to demonstrate your awareness of health and safety considerations and how they impact on make-up and hair design. See the section on health and safety for more information about this.

DON'T FORGET

You must document the process of designing make-up and hair for a production in your support log. Include initial ideas, designs, trial make-up photographs and any problems or changes you had to make.

VIDEO LINK

The video at www.brightredbooks.net/N5Drama is useful for learning about highlighting and shading.

ONLINE TEST

How well have you learned this topic? Take the test at www.brightredbooks.net/N5Drama

PROBLEM-SOLVING

Creating a production is an extended exercise in problem-solving and each member of the production team will come across issues that they need to resolve. This is part of the fun of theatre and provides an opportunity to be creative. One strategy to help with problem-solving is to think ahead and be prepared. Have a look at the ideas in the problem-solving section (pp 40–41).

THINK AHEAD

As you go through the process of developing a performance, always look ahead and try to foresee problems that might arise. Whatever your role in the production, forewarned is forearmed and if you have already thought about it and have a plan or strategy, it might not be a problem at all.

ACTING

Possible problems	Possible solutions
Forgetting lines	Start learning them early. Have prompters?
Corpsing	Practise improvising in that situation.
Illness	Look after yourself well, drink plenty of water and get plenty of sleep.
Losing your voice	Rest your voice. Have throat lozenges ready.

SET DESIGN

Possible problems	Possible solutions
Not able to get what you need to make the set	Think laterally. Can you suggest location another way? Consider using projections, shapes or just one symbolic item like a post box or a lamp post.
The set doesn't fit on the stage	Measure accurately when designing. Check the measurements and that parts of the set fit as you expected during the build. Have the set ready at least two weeks before the performance so you have time for adjustments.
Set damaged or falling apart	Have a tool kit backstage for emergency repairs. Gaffer tape is extremely useful!
Doors won't open	Check your set before every rehearsal and performance so you can catch problems like this before they happen.

LIGHTING DESIGN

Possible problems	Possible solutions
Programming fails	If your pre-programmed cues don't work, you will have to operate each cue manually. Make sure your cue sheet details all the information you need for this.
Lights don't work	Check all your lanterns before each performance, flashing through all the lights. Have spare bulbs and fuses ready. If you can't solve the problem, put the house lights up so the performance can continue.

SOUND DESIGN

Possible problems	Possible solutions
Sound equipment fails	Check your equipment before each performance and have spare fuses ready.
Microphones not working	Do a sound check before each performance and test all microphones. Have spare microphones available.

contd

PROPS

Possible problems	Possible solutions
Lost props	Make sure you have a master props list and check everything is there before every performance. Have spares of small, easily lost items.
Broken props	Have a tool kit backstage for emergency repairs. Make sure it includes tape, glue, string, scissors, screws and a screwdriver.

COSTUME DESIGN

Possible problems	Possible solutions
Can't get costumes you need	Think laterally. Can you do it a different way? Perhaps you could have all the characters in one plain colour and suggest character with one item like a hat or a handbag?
Lost costume	Have a costume list and check that the items are all present before each performance. Insist that actors change after a performance and do not take costumes home. Have a box of spare items in a similar style for emergencies.
Stuck zips	If it's stuck when an actor is removing it for a costume change, cut it and fix it afterwards. If it's stuck when an actor is putting it on, pin it. Wherever possible, don't use zips. Replace zips with velcro.
Damaged costume	Have a sewing kit that contains spare buttons, scissors, needles, safety pins and body tape for emergency repairs during rehearsals and the performance.

MAKE-UP AND HAIR

Possible problems	Possible solutions
An actor has an allergic reaction	Make a list of all cast allergies before rehearsals begin. Do a trial run of all make-up before the performance. If there is still a reaction, have plenty of hypo-allergenic wipes available, get the actor to wash their face thoroughly and make sure you know who the first aider is in school.
Wigs falling off	Practise regularly with wigs so you know what they need to stay on. Have plenty of hairgrips with you backstage.
Prosthetics falling off	Have an emergency tool kit backstage including spirit gum and nose putty.

 THINGS TO DO AND THINK ABOUT

A major constraint of any school performance will be resources. The production team could have loads of brilliant and creative ideas, but there will be very limited resources to make them happen. Remember that there is always a solution if you are creative enough. Think about making the things you don't have or using symbols to represent things. You can suggest location with just one item like a lamp or an umbrella.

DON'T FORGET

Problem-solving is a major part of the National 5 Drama course so make sure you document any problems you encounter and how you solved them.

 ONLINE

There is some inspiration for creating a big production with a small budget at www.brightredbooks.net/N5Drama

 ONLINE TEST

What have you learned about problem-solving? Take the test at www.brightredbooks.net/N5Drama

HEALTH AND SAFETY

A theatre production can be a dangerous thing to do but that is no reason not to do it! You just have to be aware of the risks you are taking and think about the consequences. Whatever your role in the production, you have a responsibility to keep yourself and others safe.

BE RESPONSIBLE

Be responsible. Be aware of any health and safety issues, the risks they could involve and how you can either prevent them or be prepared for them.

ACTORS

If you are performing in a very physical production, warm up properly and safely. This will help to avoid injuries such as muscle pulls and strains.

Choreograph and practise any movement sequences thoroughly so you are confident that any contact you have with others is safe. This applies particularly to fight scenes.

Check that any weapons are in good condition and don't present a risk.

Make sure also that you warm up your voice, to avoid strains and voice loss.

LIGHTING DESIGNER

If you are a lighting designer, you must demonstrate an understanding of health and safety when operating lighting equipment. Avoid working at height. Leave this to the people at school or college who are specially insured to work at height.

Ensure that **safety chains** are attached to all lanterns and avoid lifting anything heavy by yourself.

Do not work with electrical equipment alone, in case of accidents.

Warn the audience before the performance if you are using strobes, pyrotechnics or other special effects that could cause alarm.

SET DESIGNER

As with the lighting designer, do not work at height. If you are involved in building elements of set and scenery, they should be lowered to ground level for the work to be completed.

Be aware of safe working practices when working with tools, and do not lift anything heavy by yourself.

Do not move items of set and scenery or work with tools alone in case of accidents.

SOUND DESIGNER

You must demonstrate an awareness of safety when working with electrical equipment. Make sure cables are not trip hazards and that everything is turned off after rehearsals and the performance.

PROPS MANAGER

It is essential that props are organised and tidy backstage. Props that are lying around randomly in the dark result in accidents.

Keep your **props table** under control and make sure that you can see where everything is. Props should be kept in good order, so that they don't break or cause injury when they are used.

contd

COSTUME DESIGNER

You must ensure that costumes backstage are organised and that rails are stable and not causing an obstruction. Piles of discarded costumes can be a trip hazard, particularly backstage in the dark. Take safety issues into account in your designs and ensure that performers are not likely to trip over overlong costumes or be restricted in their movements.

MAKE-UP DESIGNER

As the make-up designer for a show, you have to consider allergy and hygiene issues. Use hypo-allergenic products wherever possible. Have specific brushes and sponges for each actor and clean them between each use. Pay attention to use-by dates on cosmetics and store them safely.

DON'T FORGET

It is important to show an awareness of health and safety issues in your support log.

ONLINE

There is a useful link about health and safety in hair and makeup design at www.brightredbooks.net/N5Drama

BACKSTAGE SAFETY IS EVERYONE'S RESPONSIBILITY

Some health and safety issues are everyone's responsibility. For example, be aware of the general backstage area whether you are on a stage or using a classroom or studio. It should be organised and tidy with space for people to move around. Make sure everyone can see backstage. Often a dim blue light is used for cast and crew to be able to see backstage, but check it cannot be seen by the audience.

There should also be a first aid kit backstage. Everyone needs to know who the first aider is.

ONLINE

This information is aimed at professional theatre, but you can find health and safety information on every aspect of theatre production at www.brightredbooks.net/N5Drama

THINGS TO DO AND THINK ABOUT

Create a list in your support log of all the health and safety risks you need to consider for your role. Make sure you consider these as you are developing your performance and mention how you are going to address them.

Stay safe!

ONLINE TEST

How well have you learned this topic? Take the test at www.brightredbooks.net/N5Drama

ASSESSMENT

ANALYSING/WATCHING DRAMA

Watch as many examples of different drama **forms** and **styles** as you can throughout the course. This will improve your knowledge and experience of drama and will give you a great background to draw upon when you are devising your own drama. If you can't see a live theatre performance, make use of online video resources or DVDs.

It is very useful to see different productions of the same play, because you can compare the elements and analyse the choices that have been made by the director and cast. For example, try to see a traditional and a modern production of the same Shakespeare play and think about which you prefer and why.

VIDEO LINK

Watch the clip of the director and cast of the Royal Shakespeare Company's *Midsummer Night's Dream* discussing the choices that were made and why at www.brightredbooks.net/N5Drama

THINGS TO CONSIDER

THE SET AND STAGING

What choices have been made about the staging? Why do you think the director has chosen this? What effect does it have on the production and on the audience? For example, if there is a **proscenium arch** stage, the audience will be quite removed from the action, whereas if the staging is **theatre in the round**, the audience will be more involved in the action.

Consider the set, too. Is it an elaborate set that creates a visual backdrop for the action or is the set very minimal so that the audience have to imagine the rest?

The set designer will have worked with the director on creating a certain effect through their design. For example, a set for a play such as Samuel Becket's *Waiting for Godot* might be very sparse and minimal to create an atmosphere of desolation and loneliness, whereas a set for big West End musical will be much more elaborate to create a spectacle and sense of awe. A Noel Coward play such as *Blithe Spirit* will probably require a more realistic set as a backdrop to the action, because it is a domestic drama.

A set from *Waiting for Godot*

A set from *Blithe Spirit*

LIGHTING AND SOUND

Think about how the lighting affects the mood and atmosphere of the show. Is it effective or distracting? Is the lighting stylised and theatrical or realistic? Are sound effects used? What about other production elements such as smoke or special effects?

contd

THE STYLE OF ACTING

Is the style of acting **melodramatic** or **naturalistic**? Do you believe in the characters that are being presented? For example, are they deliberately being presented as absurd or as stereotypes as in pantomime?

THE STRUCTURE OF THE NARRATIVE

Is time linear in the piece or is it non-linear with **flashbacks** and **flashforwards**? How does this affect the flow and pace of the action? Is the structure difficult to follow or does it make it more interesting? How has this been managed in the production? How do we know that the timeline has changed?

Some productions use a different media to differentiate timelines – for example, the flashback scenes are presented as film, or lighting techniques are used to show the timeline has changed.

TECHNIQUES AND CONVENTIONS

Is there a narrator? Why do you think this is? Do the actors speak directly to the audience? Is there any audience participation? How do these techniques affect you as an audience? Do you feel more involved?

VOICE AND MOVEMENT

How do the actors use voice, body language and movement around the stage? Is there anything special or unusual about how this is used? Is there dance involved in the performance and how does this add to or enhance the show?

CONTRAST AND PLACE

Try to identify if there are some scenes that are slower and more dialogue-focused and some that involve more action. Is there any kind of pattern to this? What kind of effect do you think it creates? Is the action fast-paced and frantic or is it a more calm and thoughtful experience? Is the action broken up with dialogue or calmer sections?

YOUR REACTION TO THE DRAMA

Whether you have enjoyed the experience or not, try to identify what it was that influenced your reaction. How did it make you feel? If you were bored, what would have made it more exciting for you? Was there a particular part of the production that affected you the most?

THINGS TO DO AND THINK ABOUT

Write a review. Although it is not a requirement for passing National 5 Drama, it allows you to practise your critical evaluation skills and can help with thinking about how certain techniques and ideas might work for your own productions.

Imagine you are reviewing the play for a newspaper to let readers know if the show is worth going to see. Justify all your statements and opinions about the show by providing evidence. Read some reviews first to get a feel for the language and the way they are structured.

Keep a record in your log book of all the productions you have seen. Try to include a short paragraph on all the headings listed above for every production you see. Once you are used to this process, you could start to add in your own headings.

Discuss your thoughts with others who have seen the production. They might see things in a different way, which could add to your analysis of the production.

SELECTING A TEXT

You have to select a text for your externally assessed performance, so it makes sense to practise responding to a text during your course.

When selecting a text for performance, consider all the implications of your choice. Let's have a look at some of these.

OPPORTUNITIES

Choose a play that offers both performers and the production team the opportunity to respond creatively.

You should also choose a play that offers opportunities to explore **characterisation** and relationships in depth because this will give you more scope to demonstrate your knowledge and skill.

CONTEXT

You have to demonstrate an understanding of the social, cultural and historical context of the play, so it's a good idea to choose a play from an era that you either know something about or that appeals to you.

CAST

The number of characters is a major consideration. Think about how many performers you have and the size of the cast for the script. Some performers might be able to double up and play more than one role, but make sure they have time for a costume change if necessary.

BE SENSITIVE

Are there any issues in the text that might cause offence? Some older texts might be offensive to modern sensibilities. Attitudes have changed particularly towards race, gender and sexuality. This doesn't mean that you should avoid any texts that deal with these issues or include politically sensitive material, because they can be interesting and challenging – just be aware that you will need to approach them sensitively.

THINK ABOUT TIME

If it needs a significant amount of work, do you have time? Be realistic about the amount of time you have to work on a production. Simple is usually best, so don't overstretch yourself. There are many short plays that can be staged simply and effectively, or you could perform an extract.

STAGING

There are always options but if it needs certain elements to work, do you have the technical capabilities? Think carefully about **staging** in terms of the space and facilities you have available. If the text requires elaborate set and lighting, do you have the necessary facilities? Can you stage the play in a minimal way and still make it work?

FAMOUS VS UNKNOWN

Selecting a well-known text can make it difficult to break with tradition, but it also provides an opportunity to see how others have managed. You will have many references to draw upon to inform your own production and will be able to watch videos of other productions and read different interpretations of the script. While this can be useful, it can also make it quite challenging to present a new approach or to even imagine another interpretation.

Selecting a less well-known text could mean that there will be less to draw upon in terms of research, but it will also allow more creative freedom for your own interpretation of the text.

DON'T FORGET

You must not simply copy what you have seen in another production. It is fine to use examples as inspiration, but you must present your own interpretation.

GENRE

Think about the genre you would like to perform. Challenge yourself to try a genre you have not tackled before.

AUDIENCE

You will also need to consider your audience. Who will your audience be and what kind of production would appeal to them? There would be little point in choosing a text with adult themes for young children, and vice versa. If the audience is going to be mainly older people, consider texts that they might have a personal relationship with, or that would be nostalgic for them.

THINGS TO DO AND THINK ABOUT

Read through a range of texts with your group before you make a choice. Experiment with different interpretations and see which captures your imagination the most.

Make a shortlist of perhaps three texts and workshop them for a session. Practise some rehearsal techniques (such as hot-seating or improvisation) with extracts of each text and see which offers the most scope or which you 'click' with.

Devise a voting system to make sure that the decision is fair and that no members of the group feel marginalised. For example, if you have a shortlist of three, give each member of the group six sticky dots. Make sure that everyone either has the same colour or everyone has a mixture of colours. Each member must stick three dots on their first choice, two on their second choice and one on their third choice. The text with the most dots is the most preferred choice.

Keep a record of your discussions and the decision process in your support log. This is an important element of your performance assessment and demonstrates the thinking behind the choice of text. Include all the reasons for choosing the text, and any reservations you might have or problems you foresee, as this will demonstrate your ability to solve problems.

DON'T FORGET

Discuss interpretations of a text with others. There are often many ways to interpret meaning and this will help you to see the alternatives.

ONLINE TEST

Take the 'Selecting a Text' test online at www.brightredbooks.net/N5Drama

RESPONDING TO A TEXT

Once you have chosen a text, you have to analyse it in detail to develop your response to it. There are endless ways to interpret and present every text, which is why every theatre production you see will be different. That is part of the joy of drama. When you are creating your performance you need to consider a number of decisions.

AUDIENCE

There is no point to a performance without an audience: they are crucial to the production. Who will the audience for this play be? Will it appeal to children, families, teenagers, older people or women? Your approach will be informed by the audience.

KEY THEMES

Decide what the overall intention/message of the play is. What staging solutions will get this across most effectively to an audience? What style of acting will be suitable and why? For example, you might want the audience to feel the loneliness and isolation of an outsider, or the threat and energy of an urban setting. You might want them to leave uplifted by hope, or thoughtful about the moral of the story. Whatever your intention is, you need to keep this in mind when creating your performance.

VIDEO LINK

Watch the clip about the importance of a detailed reading of the text at www.brightredbooks.net/N5Drama

RESEARCH

Do some background research. If it is a well-known text, you will be able to access a wealth of information about how others have approached it and their reasoning behind this. If it is less well-known, you will need to research the time period and/or the culture that it is set in. Research is important because it could contribute to understanding how your character behaves or what the costumes or set should look like.

You could decide to update a historical play and set it in modern times to show how a central theme is relevant today. If you are doing this, however, you should still demonstrate an awareness of the **social and cultural context** of the play, and be able to explain why you chose to update it. You could also include references to the historical context in costume or props for example.

ANNOTATE

Read the text carefully and **annotate** sections that you think require further explanation. Mark up any parts that you do not fully understand. You should also make notes about your thoughts on the motivations of, and relationships between, characters. If you have been cast as a performer, you should look at your character's dialogue and relationships in detail, and make notes about possible ways to portray that character and their emotions.

If you have taken on a production role, you will need to annotate with this in mind. With costume, for example, you should consider the historical context and the fashions of the time, as well as how to design costumes to portray the character, mood and tone of the piece.

contd

You also need to think about physical requirements and restrictions. The type of movement required by a character, or use of props, might dictate certain costume decisions. For example, if a character is required to be quite active and perform an action or fight sequence, the costume will need to be flexible so it doesn't restrict the actor's movements.

DON'T FORGET

You can also include your annotated script in your support log.

THE FOUR 'WS'

When you are annotating the script it will be useful to start by asking yourself the four 'Ws': when, where, why and what?

WHEN?

When is it set? Is it set in a historical time period? Is it set in a particular time of day? Does it need a **flashback**? Make sure you are aware of this for each scene.

WHERE?

Where is it set? What country or region? This could be significant for costume and set design or accent. Also, does the action move about between scenes and will you need different sets to portray this?

WHY?

Why do the characters behave as they do? Are there cultural or social conventions or pressures affecting their behaviour? For example, women in Victorian times would act and speak very differently from today. Also, the relationships between characters will affect behaviour. You must consider the context.

DON'T FORGET

Remember to document all your thoughts, discussions and decisions about your approach to the text in your support log.

WHAT?

What do the actors do to demonstrate meaning to the audience? If the character is agitated and feeling trapped, how will they show this? If there is unspoken resentment between characters, how will their behaviour show this?

Chart the action/narrative of the text by drawing a plot diagram or graph. This is a visual demonstration of the level of tension in a narrative. It will help with rehearsing the scenes and getting the rhythm and pace of the production right. Start with a simple diagram and add more detail as rehearsals proceed.

ONLINE

Find more information about creating a plot diagram at www.brightredbooks.net/N5Drama

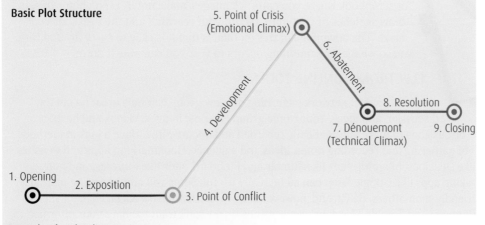

Basic Plot Structure

1. Opening
2. Exposition
3. Point of Conflict
4. Development
5. Point of Crisis (Emotional Climax)
6. Abatement
7. Dénouemont (Technical Climax)
8. Resolution
9. Closing

Example of a plot diagram

ONLINE TEST

Try out the 'Responding to a Text' test online at www.brightredbooks.net/N5Drama

THINGS TO DO AND THINK ABOUT

Do a group reading of the text and discuss other people's responses to it. Try reading the characters in different ways with different actors. This will help you to see the possibilities for interpreting the story and the characters.

RECORDING EVIDENCE

Recording evidence is an essential aspect of National 5 Drama because it shows evidence of your development and learning. You will be assessed on your preparation for performance. This is worth 10 marks, so it is worth getting into the habit of gathering evidence and using a support log or something similar before your assessed performance. Think of it like a diary and try to communicate with it regularly.

WHAT IS IT?

Overall, your support log should:

- include evidence that demonstrates knowledge and understanding of a variety and range of drama skills through devising original drama

- demonstrate a considered and critical response to text as an actor

- include evidence of self-evaluation and evaluation of other people's work

- include evidence of knowledge and understanding of a variety of drama production skills and how these skills enhance the presentation of drama

- show an ongoing reflective process.

This support log could take the form of video recordings, blogs, written work, interviews, a learning log, social networks or a combination of all of these. You could decide with your group or teacher what the best format will be for you.

THINGS TO CONSIDER

PAPER-BASED DIARIES

Keep a log book like a diary and write in it after every rehearsal, lesson and even whenever an idea comes to you. This could be like a sketchbook or scrapbook where you can stick images, make notes, keep photos of sets, draw sketches of costumes, record your research and the decisions you make. The advantage of this method is that it is easy to carry around with you so whenever something occurs to you, you can note it down.

ELECTRONIC/ONLINE TOOLS

A private social network page, blog or Glow group can be a great forum for discussion and ideas. Your whole group can post images, videos and have discussions that are automatically recorded and documented. Have a look at methods of gathering and recording notes, ideas and evidence. Bookmarking apps and websites like Delicious, blogging sites like Tumblr and Pinboard, sites like Pinterest and note-taking apps like Google Keep can all be really useful. Some will appeal and be more user-friendly than others. Be careful, however, with those that have a social element such as Pinterest and Tumblr. Check privacy settings if you don't want to share your information.

BE ORGANISED

Whatever format you use, try to be organised and create folders or sections for similar things. This will help when you are preparing for your exam and when you are looking back over your notes. If you prefer a paper-based method, use a folder or ring binder so you can rearrange things easily.

ONLINE

Head to www.
brightredbooks.net/N5Drama
for a full list of links to the
online tools mentioned here.

WHAT TO RECORD

Your support log will probably have a different structure for different stages of the process of developing a production. At the beginning of the process, when you are developing ideas, it will need to include details of the following:

- the stimulus or section of the play you are using
- research notes with sources
- initial ideas
- ideas that are rejected and the reasons why
- ideas that are selected for further development
- ideas about themes, plot, characters, setting
- details of the audience for your performance
- production concepts
- problems encountered and possible solutions
- final selection of idea and the reasons why

Once you start rehearsals, this support log will become more of a rehearsal diary. Use this to reflect upon and evaluate your progress and that of the drama. This should include:

- the aim of the rehearsal
- self-evaluation
- peer evaluation
- further development ideas.

There is further support and information about self- and peer evaluation in the section on 'reflecting and evaluating' (pp 38–39).

THINGS TO DO AND THINK ABOUT

Get into the habit of reflecting on and evaluating every rehearsal. Give yourself 10 minutes at the end of each session to write down or video log your thoughts about how it went. You can always add to it later once you have had some time to reflect further, but it's important to write your initial thoughts down right away so you have something to expand on. Don't leave it too long to do this.

Think about the format for your support log. Discuss this with your teacher to help you to make a decision. Think about how you need to use it. Do you need to take it to every drama session and rehearsal? Should it be something you can add to constantly? If you are using a tablet, you could record everything electronically as you can record rehearsals and discussions, note down thoughts or bookmark websites for research on one device. Think about how you could gather this together for the external assessor.

Experiment with different ways of recording evidence and documenting your learning to find what you are most comfortable with. It won't take long for you to discover what is the most useful and convenient for you.

DON'T FORGET

This list is not exhaustive. You and your teacher will have ideas for other things that you might need to include.

DON'T FORGET

Your support log is a learning tool. It will be really helpful if you are honest and open in your reflections and evaluations.

ONLINE TEST

Test yourself on 'Recording evidence – support log' at www.brightredbooks.net/ N5Drama

PERFORMANCE

Assessment for National 5 Drama will take various forms. To be awarded the qualification you must pass both the written and performance elements of the assessment.

Part of your assessment will include your ongoing documentation of your preparation for performance so it important you keep a record of this. You will also sit a written exam and give a performance, which will be assessed by a visiting assessor. Information about the written exam can be found on pp 94–95.

PERFORMANCE REQUIREMENTS

There are two parts to the assessed performance – this applies whether you are in a performing or in a production role. The performance itself is worth 50 marks and the support log – called **preparation for performance** – is worth 10 marks.

In the performance you should aim to:
- demonstrate your skills, knowledge and understanding to create and develop a creative concept for a performance from a text as either an actor or in a production role
- apply your knowledge and understanding of a text to your chosen production area in a performance
- apply skills in problem-solving to work collaboratively with others to create and present a drama performance from a text.

CHOOSING THE TEXT

Your teacher might decide on the extract for your assessed performance, or you and your group might have the opportunity to choose this. You should think about all the members of your group and their chosen production role, and ensure that the text you choose gives everyone the opportunity to fulfil the necessary requirements.

SUGGESTED TEXTS

These are just suggestions – you can choose other texts.
- An adapted version of *Tally's Blood* by Anne Marie Di Mambro.
- An adaptation of *Passing Places* by Stephen Greenhorn.
- An adaptation of *Blood Brothers* by Willie Russell.
- Extracts from *The Steamie* by Tony Roper.
- Extracts from *Bold Girls* by Rona Munro.
- *The Effect of Gamma Rays on Man-in-the-moon Marigolds* by Paul Zindel.
- *Shakers* by John Godber and Jane Thornton.
- *Bouncers* by John Godber.
- *Our Day Out* by Willie Russell.
- *A Night Out* by Harold Pinter.

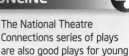

ONLINE

The National Theatre Connections series of plays are also good plays for young people and can be bought through the link at www.brightredbooks.net/N5Drama

WHAT ARE THEY LOOKING FOR?

ACTING

If you have chosen an acting role, your performance must have a minimum of two and a maximum of ten actors, and last between 10 and 50 minutes, depending on the number of people performing. It is not essential that everyone in your performance is being assessed so you can ask students from other classes to help you if you need more actors. In your performance, you need to demonstrate that you can respond to a text, interpret character, sustain a character and apply effective use of voice and movement in a performance.

contd

If you choose to take on a production role, you will take part in the performance by providing lighting, sound, costumes, make-up and hair, props or set, and the assessor will check your notes, designs, cue sheets, lists, photographs and any other evidence you have collected. They will also watch you demonstrate your skill before or during the performance.

COSTUME DESIGNER

As the costume designer, you must provide costumes for all characters in the performance. One costume should be made or altered in detail to reflect the style of the drama, the character being portrayed and to fit the actor. You should also have detailed costume designs and a **costume list** for all characters in the play. You must maintain, store and label all the costumes appropriately in preparation for the performance and fit and check the costumes on the actors before they go on stage.

LIGHTING DESIGNER

The **lighting rig** for the assessed performance must include no less than eight **lanterns**. There should be at least seven **lighting cues** used and five different **lighting states**. You must design the lighting states and produce a detailed **lighting plot** and a **cue sheet**. You must **rig** (or instruct someone to rig) the lanterns that you need and **focus** them using the correct **gels**. You must carry out a pre-show check and operate the lighting for the performance according to your cue sheet.

MAKE-UP AND HAIR DESIGNER

As the make-up and hair designer, you should apply at least one full make-up and hair for the performance and produce designs for all the other characters. Your

designs and the applied make-up should reflect character requirements and the style of the drama. You should demonstrate an awareness of health and safety and use appropriate materials and tools safely and hygienically.

PROPS MANAGER

If you are in charge of props for the performance, you must provide a minimum of eight different props. They should be a variety of **costume**, **set** and **personal props**. You should design and create one fully functional prop for the assessed performance, create a **master props list** and organise the **props table** for the performance. You must also show that you can label and store the props effectively.

SET DESIGNER

As the set designer for the performance, you must produce working designs and plans for the set. Include a detailed **ground plan** and an **elevation** that is appropriate for the text and **design concept**. The final set should reflect your design and be functional in performance. You must also carry out pre-show checks to ensure the set is ready and safe for the performance.

SOUND DESIGNER

The sound design for the assessed performance must include at least six different sound effects and eight sound cues. You must source and edit all sounds and music for the performance, complete pre-show checks and have a backup plan in case of equipment failure. You should produce a cue sheet detailing the volume and duration of each sound cue and operate the sound for the performance according to your cue sheet.

PREPARATION FOR PERFORMANCE

As part of the performance element of the assessment, you are required to produce a written response which shows your **preparation for the performance**. There are 10 marks available for this.

The preparation for performance is carried out over a period of time. You should start this at an appropriate point in the course, in advance of the performance date. In this piece of writing, you should try to give an overview of the process you went through to develop the performance.

If you have chosen a production role, you can use your support log to record your designs and drawings.

In the 'preparation for performance' paper, marks will be awarded for:
- demonstrating your research into the chosen text
- your interpretation of the acting or production role
- your thoughts and ideas for the performance and production concept
- the development of your thoughts and ideas through rehearsals

 DON'T FORGET

Your work on the two units throughout the course will prepare you for this performance. By the time you reach this stage, you will have practised all of these skills and be feeling confident.

 THINGS TO DO AND THINK ABOUT

If you are in a production role, you will be required to demonstrate your skill and might be asked questions to clarify points of your design. So, for example, if you are designing make-up, practise doing a make-up demonstration in front of an audience. Talk about what you are doing and why, and how the design reflects the character it is designed for.

QUESTION PAPER

For National 5 Drama, your final course assessment is decided by a question paper and a performance marked by an external assessor. The question paper is marked out of 60 but is worth 40% of the award. The performance makes up the other 60%.

WHAT ARE THEY LOOKING FOR?

The questions in the exam paper could be about any of the areas you have studied throughout your course, so be prepared to answer questions about:

- characterisation
- performance or design concepts
- presenting
- audience reaction
- reflection and evaluation skills

- genre and themes
- mood and atmosphere
- rehearsal techniques
- target audience
- a range of production areas

- different staging, settings and styles of production
- problem-solving and critical thinking
- responding to stimuli.

The question paper is designed to give you an opportunity to apply the knowledge and understanding you have developed through the course and show that you can describe and evaluate your own and other people's performances. It will also test your ability to describe the ways in which you would apply your skills

and knowledge to a performance, either as an actor or as part of a production team.

The question paper has two sections. Section One asks you to evaluate your own performance and Section Two asks for a creative response to a stimuli.

SECTION ONE – EVALUATING YOUR PERFORMANCE

The first section of the paper will be about a production that you have taken part in – either in an acting or in a production role. You can choose any production that you have worked on during your course.

The questions will ask you about the experience you have had and encourage you to be evaluative and reflective.

You should describe your experience and reflect back on the reasons for your decisions and how effective your choices were. You must use appropriate vocabulary in your response to demonstrate your knowledge and understanding of the drama and production skills you have used and developed.

EXAMPLE QUESTIONS

> **EXAMPLE:**
>
> 1. Who would be the ideal target audience for your drama? Explain your answer. (2)
>
> The important thing to note about this question is that it has two parts and two marks available. If you only state who the target audience is and do not explain why, you will only get one of the marks. If the question asks you to explain, you must do so. Try to give more than one reason to give yourself the best possible chance of getting both marks. You should also make sure your answer is positive and don't mention who would not be an ideal audience. So a good response would be:
>
> > The target audience for this drama would be teenagers. This is because the main characters are teenagers so the audience would be able to identify with them. It also deals with issues and themes that teenagers are interested in like popularity and bullying. The performance used current popular music that would appeal to that age group and references to TV programmes that teenagers might watch.
>
> This response answered the question by stating the target audience (teenagers) and giving three reasons why (identifying with characters, interesting themes and age appropriate references).

There might also be longer questions such as:

contd

2. Evaluate the effectiveness of your final performance.

If you were in an **acting role**, you should include comments on performance concepts and the mood/ atmosphere created.

Or

If you were in a **production role**, you should include comments on design concepts and the mood/ atmosphere created. (6)

Note that this question has six marks available, so you must make at least six good points to get all of the marks. The question asks you to evaluate, so you must comment on aspects of your final performance that you thought worked well and those that were not so effective. You must also explain why.

SECTION TWO – CREATIVE RESPONSE

Section Two of the paper will ask you to respond creatively to an unseen stimulus. This could be any number of things including a photograph, a poem, an image of an object or a piece of text. You will be asked to suggest ideas on story, characters, setting and plot. You should offer a range of ideas as to how this devised drama could be presented in terms of style and form. This might include ideas for a production concept such as lighting, sound and costume ideas, conventions and techniques and how to communicate ideas effectively to an audience.

EXAMPLE QUESTIONS

3. Choose one of the stimuli above and answer the questions on your chosen stimulus.
   (a) Describe a time period in which you would set your drama and explain your choice. (2)

As with the questions in Section One, it is important to look at the number of marks available and answer accordingly. This question asks you to describe and then explain. You will get one mark for each. Again, try to give more than one reason to make sure you get both marks. For example:

> I would set the drama in the 1950s and the present time. This is because the letter is about a relationship that the writer had 50 years ago, so there could be flashbacks. It would be interesting for an audience to give them a window into a different time and it would mean some interesting costumes and music could be used.

This answer gives the time period (1950s and present day) and gives three reasons why (it relates to the stimulus, interest for the audience and the opportunities for production elements).

There will also be more complex and longer questions in this section such as:

3. (b) Think about the purpose or message of your drama. How will the plot and setting help to communicate this purpose or message? (6)

3. (c) Name two conventions you would use in your drama and, for each one, explain the advantage of using it. (4)

4. Choose and describe a key moment in your drama. Explain why you consider it to be a key moment. (4)

For every question, look at the number of marks available and try to exceed that number with the points that you make.

 THINGS TO DO AND THINK ABOUT

Practise answering the questions in Section One for a performance you have been part of. Make sure you answer the question and then **explain** your answer. Ask a friend to do this with you and swap answers for marking. Only give marks if they have answered the question clearly and given a reason.

In the exam paper, there is a page for you to write down notes/ideas for your chosen stimulus. It is a good idea to use this as it will help you remember your ideas and give you a chance to consider your storyline/plot. This will not be marked, but will be useful for you to create your drama.

 ONLINE

There are some good examples of how to evaluate your own performance at www.brightredbooks.net/ N5Drama

...r a
... some form.
...ormers around the

... use of movements and postures
... communicate character and emotion.

...ng – the process of selecting the actors who will play the characters.

Chorus – an important aspect of Greek drama, involving many people speaking in unison.

Chracterisation – techniques used to develop a character performance.

Chronological – in linear time order.

Climax – the part of a narrative where the conflict reaches a turning point of some kind.

Commedia dell'arte – a form of fifteenth-century Italian street theatre that uses masks.

Conflict – an essential part of narrative structure that involves some kind of struggle. This contributes towards the tension in drama.

Constructive criticism – identifying what is effective and what can be improved, and how.

Contrast – creating difference between scenes to sustain pace and interest. For example, it might be the contrast between noise and silence or between action and dialogue.

Corpse – to break character while performing.

Cue – this is a signal for a sound effect to begin or end, a lighting change, a line to be spoken or for an actor to enter or exit.

Device – a technique to achieve a certain effect, like a monologue or an aside.

Dialogue – words spoken by actors onstage.

Directorial concept – an overarching theme or idea that ties the performance and production in a show together, to ensure a consistent look, feel or message.

Dramatic arc – a story structure that incorporates exposition, rising action, climax, falling action and resolution.

Dramatic tension – this raises the audience's expectations that something will happen, and creates interest.

Dress rehearsal – a rehearsal in full costume and with all technical elements.

Elevation – a set design drawing from the perspective of eye level.

End on stage – a type of staging in which the audience are all on one side of the performance area.

Entrance – a place onstage or within the set where a performer can enter the acting area, or the point in the performance at which an actor enters into the performance space.

Exit – a place onstage or within the set where a performer can leave the acting area, or the point in the performance at which an actor leaves the performance space.

Exposition – the first part of a narrative that introduces the characters and sets the scene.

Expressionism – a style of theatre from Germany involving stark and angled sets and alienating techniques.

Eye contact – a method of communication using the eyes and involving intense focus between performers or the audience.

Facial expression – use of the facial features to communicate emotion.

Fade in – bringing in sound slowly, while increasing the volume.

Fade out – slowly decreasing the volume of a sound until it stops.

Falling action – the part of a narrative following the climax, when problems begin to be solved and questions are answered.

Farce – a subgenre of comedy involving ridiculous situations and characters.

Fast fade – fading lighting out quickly.

Fixed mask – a mask with a certain character or expression.

Flashbacks – a narrative technique, involving jumps backwards in time to show events leading up to the ...esent.

...shforwards – a narrative technique involving jumps ...ard in time.

... – directing the audience's attention to a ...lar area of the stage or performance area.

... a category of theatre with certain ...ristics like physical theatre or pantomime.

...urth wall – an imaginary wall between the performers and the audience.

Genre – a category of drama specific to the type of story that is being told – for example, comedy or tragedy.

Gesture – small movements of the head or hands that communicate meaning.

Greek drama – an ancient form of theatre. They are usually tragedies, written by playwrights such as Sophocles.

Green room – an area backstage for actors to wait in when not on stage.

Ground plan – a bird's-eye view of the set, showing furniture, entrances/exits and the position of the audience.

Hot-seating – interviewing a character in role.

Immersive theatre – a form of theatre, like promenade theatre, where the audience walk through the performance area and can become involved in the action.

Improvisation – a technique that involves performers creating drama with no prior discussion or planning.

Improvisational theatre – an unscripted form of theatre using only improvisation.

Levels – the use of the body to occupy different levels in movement.

Lighting state – a particular configuration of lights to be used in a section of a production.

Linear – a narrative structure involving events that happen in chronological order.

Long-form improvisation – a sub-genre of improvisational theatre where performers create a sustained piece of theatre with no prior planning.

Marking – positions that are marked with tape on the set or stage for performers.

Melodrama – a genre of drama involving over-the-top emotions and action.

Mime – a dramatic form involving a performance without the use of speech.

Modernism – a style of theatre influenced by realism and symbolism.

Monologue – a speech made by a character, as if they are speaking their thoughts to other characters or to the audience.

Motivation – the reasons behind a character's actions.

Narrator – a performer who tells part of the story directly to the audience.

Naturalistic – a style of theatre that aims to create a perfect illusion of reality.

Neutral mask – a mask with a neutral expression.

Non-linear – a narrative structure involving jumps in time forward and backwards.

Pace – the speed and rhythm of a performance or scene.

Parody – a subgenre of comedy involving an exaggerated imitation of something for comic effect.

Participatory theatre – a theatre form in which the audience can get involved and affect the action.

POSSE – a mnemonic to remember that mime should be precise, obvious, simple, slow and exaggerated.

Postmodernism – a style of theatre that concentrates on the audience creating meaning, and therefore presents more questions than answers.

Posture – the manner in which a character stands or sits.

Preparation for performance – the extended response part of the National 5 Drama assessment.

Production concept – an idea for a performance that ties everything together.

Promenade theatre – an unconventional theatre form involving the audience moving through a space during the performance.

Proscenium arch – a traditional type of stage, with an arch at the front.

Proxemics – the way in which use of space communicates status and meaning.

Rehearsal techniques – drama techniques such as swapping roles, hot seating and improvisation that are used in rehearsal to develop a performance.

Resolution – the final part of a narrative where a conclusion is reached.

Rising action – the part of a narrative that introduces some kind of conflict and begins to build tension.

Scene – a section of a play. A sequence of scenes makes an act or a play.

Short-form improvisation – a sub-genre of improvisational theatre involving improvised scenes or games.

Sight lines – an imaginary line from the audience to the performance area to show what can be seen.

Slapstick – a sub-genre of comedy that involves physical comedy such as falling over and other clumsy accidents.

Social and cultural influences – the aspects of time and place that can affect characters and the narrative of a play. Politics and religion are an example.

Social realism – a style of theatre that presents a performance as if it is reality, usually with a political message of some kind.

Soliloquy – a passage of speech made by a character, as if they are speaking their thoughts aloud but are unheard by other characters.

Split stage – this is a stage that has two or more areas to depict different locations or times. It allows you to change the location or time without a complete set or scenery change.

Staging – the way in which a performance is staged – for example, in the round or proscenium arch.

Stance – an element of body language or movement describing the way a character stands.

Status – the level of power a character has in relation to others.

Stimuli – anything that stimulates creative ideas for a performance, including text.

Strike – to remove, dismantle and store the set and scenery after a performance, or to reset the lights to a default state.

Structure – the way a story is put together. This could be linear or non-linear.

Style – the way in which a story is told – for example, naturalistic or surreal.

Stylised – something performed in a non-realistic manner.

Support log – a record in some form of the process of creating drama.

Surrealist – a style of theatre that aims to express the unconscious mind: it can be dream-like and strange.

Suspension of disbelief – the audience's willingness to forget that they are watching a performance and believe in the characters and story.

Sustaining the role – maintaining focus and staying in character throughout a performance.

T-bar – a floor stand onto which lanterns can be attached.

Tableaux/tableau – performers representing a scene or story in a frozen image.

Technical rehearsal – a rehearsal in which the technical aspects such as sound and lights are perfected.

Text – any written material including script, plays and extracts.

Theatre arts – another name for production skills such as lighting or costume design.

Theatre conventions – elements used in performance to enhance the storytelling or aid the understanding of the audience such as narration or soliloquy.

Theatre in the round – a form of staging that involves the audience being on all sides of the performance area.

Thought tracking – freezing the action during rehearsal and speaking the thoughts of a character aloud.

Thought tunnel – a characterisation or rehearsal technique that involves a group of people in two lines facing each other (the tunnel) and one person (in role) walking slowly through the tunnel. The people that form the tunnel speak their thoughts aloud.

Thrust stage – a stage that protrudes into the auditorium so that the audience is seated on three sides of the performance area.

Traverse stage – a form of staging where the audience is on either side of the performance area, facing each other.

Understudy – a performer who learns a part of another actor in case of absence on performance night.

Use of space – the way in which movement is choreographed around the performance space.

Writing in role – a characterisation technique where the actor writes a letter or a diary entry in role as the character.